101 Crossword Puzzles For Dummies™, Volume 1

Quick Reference Card

Your Crossword Solving Strategy

Try the following steps for successful solving:

1. **Locate a missing-word clue.**

    You don't need to start with the first Across clue. Keep looking for a missing-word clue until you find one — every editor includes some missing-word clues in easy-to-solve crosswords.

2. **After you enter an answer for one clue, work on the clues that connect to the clue you already answered.**

3. **Scout around for other three- or four-letter entries in the grid.**

    You may find shorter entries in corners, where Down clues are generally shorter than Across ones.

4. **Investigate one of the corners, such as the bottom-right corner.**

    The shorter entries in corners make the clues in corners generally easy to crack.

5. **Check out the mirror image of the corner that you solved.**

    After you unravel a corner of a crossword, you may find that the counterpart corner in the other half of the diagram is equally accessible.

6. **Look for theme entries.**

    Some puzzles include longer entries that are connected through a common subject. If you get the answer to one of these clues and catch on to the trick, it may help you to solve the other theme-related clues by looking for a common thread. (Themes tie together the longer entries through this subject.)

7. **Continue solving until you've successfully filled each square.**

Puzzle-Related Web Sites to Visit

If you have access to the World Wide Web, check out these great Web sites for puzzles and puzzle tips:

- **Index of Crossword Puzzles:** http://www.primate.wisc.edu/people/hamel/cp.html

- **The Los Angeles Times:** http://www.student.net/xwords

- **MacNamara's Band Crossword Puzzles:** http://www.macnamarasband.com

- **Multimedia (TV Guide):** http://www.tvguide.com/tv/xwords/htm

- **Puzzability:** http://www.puzzability.com

- **Puzzle Depot:** http://www.puzzledepot.com/index.shtml

- **Tribune Media:** http://secure.nando.net/newsroom/nnn/cross.htm

- **The Washington Post:** http://www.washingtonpost.com/wps-rv/style/longterm/cross/crossw.htm

- **Web Word Search:** http://www.geocities.com/WestHollywood/2555/puzzle.html

- **Word Puzzle of the Week:** http://www.smartcode.com/isshtml/weekwsk.htm

...For Dummies: Bestselling Book Series for Beginners

101 Crossword Puzzles For Dummies™, Volume 1

Quick Reference Card

Top Ten Three-Letter Entries That Start with E

1. EAN
2. EAT
3. EEE
4. EER
5. ENE
6. EOS
7. ERA
8. ERE
9. ERI
10. ESE

Top Ten Four-Letter Entries That Start with E

1. ECTO
2. EELY
3. EMIT
4. ENDO
5. ENOS
6. EONS
7. EPEE
8. ERIN
9. EROS
10. ETNA

Top Ten Three-Letter Entries That Start with A

1. ACE
2. ADE
3. AHA
4. ALE
5. ALP
6. ANT
7. APE
8. ARA
9. ARS
10. ASP

Top Ten Four-Letter Entries That Start with A

1. ABRI
2. ADAR
3. ADIT
4. AGAR
5. ALAI
6. ALAR
7. ALEE
8. ALOE
9. AMAH
10. AMIR

Praise for Michelle Arnot and Crossword Puzzles For Dummies

"Crosswords! Cryptograms! Acrostics! No need to be puzzled any longer. This addition to the IDG library deciphers and reveals the secrets behind the grid. You find out how puzzles are constructed, plus you get insiders' steps and hints, puzzle makers' techniques, along with sample puzzles from the top constructors. Beginners and pros alike will enjoy Michelle Arnot's insight into the world's greatest pastime. She will have you quickly join the millions of puzzlers who delight in word game addiction."
— Marilynn Huret, Editor, *At The Crosswords,*
www.atthecrossroads.com

"It is a pleasure to endorse Michelle Arnot's sprightly written book, which opens the door to the adventure and joy that is puzzle solving."
— Trude Michel Jaffe, Editor, *Los Angeles Times* Syndicate
Daily Puzzle

"Michelle Arnot is one of the clearest, liveliest, most entertaining writers in the world of puzzles. Here is an excellent beginner's guide to mastering the secrets of crosswords."
— Will Shortz, Crossword Editor, *The New York Times*

"If you're a committed puzzlehead, this book is a MUST. You've got to buy it. If you're not a puzzlehead, give your brain a break — an enchanting workout. Develop your vocabulary, impress your friends, and live happily forevermore!!"
— Thomas H. Middleton, Double Acrostics Constructor,
The New York Times and *Harper's Magazine*

"Michelle Arnot's *Crossword Puzzles For Dummies* seduces newcomers into cruciverbalsm and entertains acrossionados with a clear but comprehensive approach to the subject. She writes with authority about the culture and history of crossword puzzles from their origins to where you can find them today on the Web, gives helpful advice for solving various styles of American and British puzzles, and tests your skills with quizzes and sample puzzles. This is a great book!"
— John J. Chew, III, Chairman, National SCRABBLE® Association
Dictionary Committee, www.math.utoronto.ca/jjchew

"I give a hearty bravo to *Crossword Puzzles For Dummies*. I especially enjoyed Chapter 13, "Deciphering the Cryptic Crossword," and encourage everyone of all ages to check it out."
— Frank W. Lewis, "Setter" for the *Nation* Cryptic Crossword

TM

References for the Rest of Us!™

BUSINESS AND GENERAL REFERENCE BOOK SERIES FROM IDG

Do you find that traditional reference books are overloaded with technical details and advice you'll never use? Do you postpone important life decisions because you just don't want to deal with them? Then our *...For Dummies*™ business and general reference book series is for you.

...For Dummies business and general reference books are written for those frustrated and hard-working souls who know they aren't dumb, but find that the myriad of personal and business issues and the accompanying horror stories make them feel helpless. *...For Dummies* books use a lighthearted approach, a down-to-earth style, and even cartoons and humorous icons to diffuse fears and build confidence. Lighthearted but not lightweight, these books are perfect survival guides to solve your everyday personal and business problems.

> *"More than a publishing phenomenon, 'Dummies' is a sign of the times."*
> — The New York Times

> *"...you won't go wrong buying them."*
> — Walter Mossberg, Wall Street Journal, on IDG's ...For Dummies™ books

> *"A world of detailed and authoritative information is packed into them..."*
> — U.S. News and World Report

Already, millions of satisfied readers agree. They have made *...For Dummies* the #1 introductory level computer book series and a best-selling business book series. They have written asking for more. So, if you're looking for the best and easiest way to learn about business and other general reference topics, look to *...For Dummies* to give you a helping hand.

101 CROSSWORD PUZZLES FOR DUMMIES,™
VOLUME 1

by Michelle Arnot

IDG BOOKS WORLDWIDE

IDG Books Worldwide, Inc.
An International Data Group Company

Foster City, CA ♦ Chicago, IL ♦ Indianapolis, IN ♦ Southlake, TX

101 Crossword Puzzles for Dummies,™ Volume 1

Published by
IDG Books Worldwide, Inc.
An International Data Group Company
919 E. Hillsdale Blvd.
Suite 400
Foster City, CA 94404
www.idgbooks.com (IDG Books Worldwide Web site)
www.dummies.com (Dummies Press Web site)

Library of Congress Catalog Card No.: 97-81243

ISBN: 0-7645-5068-3

Printed in the United States of America

10 9 8 7 6 5 4 3 2 1

1B/SW/QR/ZY/IN

Distributed in the United States by IDG Books Worldwide, Inc.

Distributed by Macmillan Canada for Canada; by Transworld Publishers Limited in the United Kingdom; by IDG Norge Books for Norway; by IDG Sweden Books for Sweden; by Woodslane Pty. Ltd. for Australia; by Woodslane Enterprises Ltd. for New Zealand; by Longman Singapore Publishers Ltd. for Singapore, Malaysia, Thailand, and Indonesia; by Simron Pty. Ltd. for South Africa; by Toppan Company Ltd. for Japan; by Distribuidora Cuspide for Argentina; by Livraria Cultura for Brazil; by Ediciencia S.A. for Ecuador; by Addison-Wesley Publishing Company for Korea; by Ediciones ZETA S.C.R. Ltda. for Peru; by WS Computer Publishing Corporation, Inc., for the Philippines; by Unalis Corporation for Taiwan; by Contemporanea de Ediciones for Venezuela; by Computer Book & Magazine Store for Puerto Rico; by Express Computer Distributors for the Caribbean and West Indies. Authorized Sales Agent: Anthony Rudkin Associates for the Middle East and North Africa.

For general information on IDG Books Worldwide's books in the U.S., please call our Consumer Customer Service department at 800-762-2974. For reseller information, including discounts and premium sales, please call our Reseller Customer Service department at 800-434-3422.

For information on where to purchase IDG Books Worldwide's books outside the U.S., please contact our International Sales department at 650-655-3200 or fax 650-655-3295.

For information on foreign language translations, please contact our Foreign & Subsidiary Rights department at 650-655-3021 or fax 650-655-3281.

For sales inquiries and special prices for bulk quantities, please contact our Sales department at 650-655-3200 or write to the address above.

For information on using IDG Books Worldwide's books in the classroom or for ordering examination copies, please contact our Educational Sales department at 800-434-2086 or fax 817-251-8174.

For press review copies, author interviews, or other publicity information, please contact our Public Relations department at 650-655-3000 or fax 650-655-3299.

For authorization to photocopy items for corporate, personal, or educational use, please contact Copyright Clearance Center, 222 Rosewood Drive, Danvers, MA 01923, or fax 978-750-4470.

is a trademark under exclusive license to IDG Books Worldwide, Inc., from International Data Group, Inc.

About the Author

A funny thing happened to **Michelle Arnot** on her way to a Master's degree in 18th century French literature at Columbia University: She ended up making a career of her hobby in crosswords. Instead of writing a thesis, Michelle constructed a crossword. When the puzzle was accepted for publication, she switched gears immediately.

Michelle has been omnipresent in the world of puzzles since the publication of her book *What's Gnu: The History of the Crossword Puzzle* (Vintage Books, 1981). She has served as Editor and Publisher of dozens of national puzzle magazines, most notably for *The Herald Tribune* and the Kappa Publishing Group. Additionally, she's taught seminars on solving for the New School For Social Research and the Learning Annex. Her editorial career gradually extended into the marketing of puzzle magazines in the direct mail arena. Michelle is also the author of *Crossword Puzzles For Dummies,* published by IDG Books Worldwide, Inc.

In her other life, Michelle is a health writer who specializes in subjects of interest to women. She's written books on topics as diverse as infertility and foot care.

When she's not at the word processor, Michelle is often found tramping the hills around Sandisfield, Massachusetts where she and her family keep busy with their 150-year-old house. An avid birdwatcher, Michelle likes to match faces to the avian references she's read about in puzzles. You can easily identify Michelle in warm weather by her T-shirt adorned with a crossword grid.

ABOUT IDG BOOKS WORLDWIDE

Welcome to the world of IDG Books Worldwide.

IDG Books Worldwide, Inc., is a subsidiary of International Data Group, the world's largest publisher of computer-related information and the leading global provider of information services on information technology. IDG was founded more than 25 years ago and now employs more than 8,500 people worldwide. IDG publishes more than 275 computer publications in over 75 countries (see listing below). More than 60 million people read one or more IDG publications each month.

Launched in 1990, IDG Books Worldwide is today the #1 publisher of best-selling computer books in the United States. We are proud to have received eight awards from the Computer Press Association in recognition of editorial excellence and three from *Computer Currents'* First Annual Readers' Choice Awards. Our best-selling *...For Dummies*® series has more than 30 million copies in print with translations in 30 languages. IDG Books Worldwide, through a joint venture with IDG's Hi-Tech Beijing, became the first U.S. publisher to publish a computer book in the People's Republic of China. In record time, IDG Books Worldwide has become the first choice for millions of readers around the world who want to learn how to better manage their businesses.

Our mission is simple: Every one of our books is designed to bring extra value and skill-building instructions to the reader. Our books are written by experts who understand and care about our readers. The knowledge base of our editorial staff comes from years of experience in publishing, education, and journalism — experience we use to produce books for the '90s. In short, we care about books, so we attract the best people. We devote special attention to details such as audience, interior design, use of icons, and illustrations. And because we use an efficient process of authoring, editing, and desktop publishing our books electronically, we can spend more time ensuring superior content and spend less time on the technicalities of making books.

You can count on our commitment to deliver high-quality books at competitive prices on topics you want to read about. At IDG Books Worldwide, we continue in the IDG tradition of delivering quality for more than 25 years. You'll find no better book on a subject than one from IDG Books Worldwide.

John Kilcullen
CEO
IDG Books Worldwide, Inc.

Steven Berkowitz
President and Publisher
IDG Books Worldwide, Inc.

*Eighth Annual
Computer Press
Awards 1992*

*Ninth Annual
Computer Press
Awards 1993*

*Tenth Annual
Computer Press
Awards 1994*

*Eleventh Annual
Computer Press
Awards 1995*

IDG Books Worldwide, Inc., is a subsidiary of International Data Group, the world's largest publisher of computer-related information and the leading global provider of information services on information technology. International Data Group publishes over 275 computer publications in over 75 countries. Sixty million people read one or more International Data Group publications each month. International Data Group's publications include: **ARGENTINA:** Buyer's Guide, Computerworld Argentina, PC World Argentina; **AUSTRALIA:** Australian Macworld, Australian PC World, Australian Reseller News, Computerworld, IT Casebook, Network World, Publish, Webmaster; **AUSTRIA:** Computerwelt Osterreich, Networks Austria, PC Tip Austria; **BANGLADESH:** PC World Bangladesh; **BELARUS:** PC World Belarus; **BELGIUM:** Data News; **BRAZIL:** Annuario de Informática, Computerworld, Connections, Macworld, PC Player, PC World, Publish, Reseller News, Supergamepower; **BULGARIA:** Computerworld Bulgaria, Network World Bulgaria, PC & MacWorld Bulgaria; **CANADA:** CIO Canada, Client/Server World, ComputerWorld Canada, InfoWorld Canada, NetworkWorld Canada, WebWorld; **CHILE:** Computerworld Chile, PC World Chile; **COLOMBIA:** Computerworld Colombia, PC World Colombia; **COSTA RICA:** PC World Centro America; **THE CZECH AND SLOVAK REPUBLICS:** Computerworld Czechoslovakia, Macworld Czech Republic, PC World Czechoslovakia; **DENMARK:** Communications World Danmark, Computerworld Danmark, Macworld Danmark, PC World Danmark, Techworld Denmark; **DOMINICAN REPUBLIC:** PC World Republica Dominicana; **ECUADOR:** PC World Ecuador; **EGYPT:** Computerworld Middle East, PC World Middle East; **EL SALVADOR:** PC World Centro America; **FINLAND:** MikroPC, Tietoverkko, Tietoviikko; **FRANCE:** Distributique, Hebdo, Info PC, Le Monde Informatique, Macworld, Reseaux & Telecoms, WebMaster France; **GERMANY:** Computer Partner, Computerwoche, Computerwoche Extra, Computerwoche FOCUS, Global Online, Macwelt, PC Welt; **GREECE:** Amiga Computing, GamePro Greece, Multimedia World; **GUATEMALA:** PC World Centro America; **HONDURAS:** PC World Centro America; **HONG KONG:** Computerworld Hong Kong, PC World Hong Kong, Publish in Asia; **HUNGARY:** ABCD CD-ROM, Computerworld Szamitastechnika, Internetto online Magazine, PC World Hungary, PC-X Magazin Hungary; **ICELAND:** Tolvuheimur PC World Island; **INDIA:** Information Communications World, Information Systems Computerworld, PC World India, Publish in Asia; **INDONESIA:** InfoKomputer PC World, Komputek Computerworld, Publish in Asia; **IRELAND:** ComputerScope, PC Live!; **ISRAEL:** Macworld Israel, People & Computers/Computerworld; **ITALY:** Computerworld Italia, Macworld Italia, Networking Italia, PC World Italia; **JAPAN:** DTP World, Macworld Japan, Nikkei Personal Computing, OS/2 World Japan, SunWorld Japan, Windows NT World, Windows World Japan; **KENYA:** PC World East African; **KOREA:** Hi-Tech Information, Macworld Korea, PC World Korea; **MACEDONIA:** PC World Macedonia; **MALAYSIA:** Computerworld Malaysia, PC World Malaysia, Publish in Asia; **MALTA:** PC World Malta; **MEXICO:** Computerworld Mexico, PC World Mexico; **MYANMAR:** PC World Myanmar; **NETHERLANDS:** Computer! Totaal, LAN Internetworking Magazine, LAN World Buyers Guide, Macworld Netherlands, Net, WebWereld; **NEW ZEALAND:** Absolute Beginners Guide and Plain & Simple Series, Computer Buyer, Computer Industry Directory, Computerworld New Zealand, MTB, Network World, PC World New Zealand; **NICARAGUA:** PC World Centro America; **NORWAY:** Computerworld Norge, CW Rapport, Datamagasinet, Financial Rapport, Kursguide Norge, Macworld Norge, Multimediaworld Norge, PC World Ekspress Norge, PC World Nettverk, PC World Norge, PC World ProduktGuide Norge; **PAKISTAN:** Computerworld Pakistan; **PANAMA:** PC World Panama; **PEOPLE'S REPUBLIC OF CHINA:** China Computer Users, China Computerworld, China InfoWorld, China Telecom World Weekly, Computer & Communication, Electronic Design China, Electronics Today, Electronics Weekly, Game Software, PC World China, Popular Computer Week, Software Weekly, Software World, Telecom World; **PERU:** Computerworld Peru, PC World Profesional Peru, PC World SoHo Peru; **PHILIPPINES:** Click!, Computerworld Philippines, PC World Philippines, Publish in Asia; **POLAND:** Computerworld Poland, Computerworld Special Report Poland, Cyber, Macworld Poland, Networld Poland, PC World Komputer; **PORTUGAL:** Cerebro/PC World, Computerworld/Correio Informático, Dealer World Portugal, Mac*In/PC*In Portugal, Multimedia World; **PUERTO RICO:** PC World Puerto Rico; **ROMANIA:** Computerworld Romania, PC World Romania, Telecom Romania; **RUSSIA:** Computerworld Russia, Mir PK, Publish, Seti; **SINGAPORE:** Computerworld Singapore, PC World Singapore, Publish in Asia; **SLOVENIA:** Monitor; **SOUTH AFRICA:** Computing SA, Network World SA, Software World SA; **SPAIN:** Communications World España, Computerworld España, Dealer World España, Macworld España, PC World España; **SRI LANKA:** Infolink PC World; **SWEDEN:** CAP&Design, Computer Sweden, Corporate Computing Sweden, Internetworld Sweden, it.branschen, Macworld Sweden, MaxiData Sweden, MikroDatorn, Natverk & Kommunikation, PC World Sweden, PCaktiv, Windows World Sweden; **SWITZERLAND:** Computerworld Schweiz, Macworld Schweiz, PCtip; **TAIWAN:** Computerworld Taiwan, Macworld Taiwan, NEW ViSiON/Publish, PC World Taiwan, Windows World Taiwan; **THAILAND:** Publish in Asia, Thai Computerworld; **TURKEY:** Computerworld Turkiye, Macworld Turkiye, Network World Turkiye, PC World Turkiye; **UKRAINE:** Computerworld Kiev, Multimedia World Ukraine, PC World Ukraine; **UNITED KINGDOM:** Acorn User UK, Amiga Action UK, Amiga Computing UK, Apple Talk UK, Computing, Macworld, Parents and Computers UK, PC Advisor, PC Home, PSX Pro, The WEB; **UNITED STATES:** Cable in the Classroom, CIO Magazine, Computerworld, DOS World, Federal Computer Week, GamePro Magazine, InfoWorld, I-Way, Macworld, Network World, PC Games, PC World, Publish, Video Event, THE WEB Magazine, and WebMaster; online webzines: JavaWorld, NetscapeWorld, and SunWorld Online; **URUGUAY:** InfoWorld Uruguay; **VENEZUELA:** Computerworld Venezuela, PC World Venezuela; and **VIETNAM:** PC World Vietnam. 3/24/97

Dedication

To my daughter Astrid Brown and the next generation of solvers.

Author's Acknowledgments

The author extends her sincere thanks to all the good people at IDG Books Worldwide and Dummies Press for creating this unique opportunity. A special thanks to Mark Butler for taking the project off the shelf, and to Heather Albright and Nickole Harris for their strenuous efforts on my behalf. Above all, thanks to my editor, the serene and supremely talented Mary Goodwin. Her insight, patience, direction, good humor, and genuine interest created a productive working relationship that made the writing and editing process easier and (almost) enjoyable. And to think there's another great lady just exactly like her in the world — she's got a twin!

Many talented constuctors provided puzzles for this book. Thanks go to Theresa Curry, Randall Hartman, Fred Piscop, Julie Hess, Marilyn Huret, Jay Sullivan, Will Shortz, Eilleen Lexau, Elizabeth Gorski, David Rosen, John Greenman, Alfio Micci, Scott Schilling, Frank Longo, Bernice Gordon, and Mike Shenk.

The game of crosswords is a journey with no specific destination. As I've traveled in the land of puzzles through the years, I've been fortunate to make the acquaintance of scores of puzzle people in all aspects of the field. These people have influenced me and generously shared their knowledge. Among the many talented editorial people, who are too numerous to list here, special thanks to Will Shortz, Stan Newman, Marilyn Huret, Trude Jaffe, and Mary Lou Tobias. Also thank you to the Kappa Publishing Group, which I've had the pleasure of being affiliated with for more than decade.

Last but not least, thanks to my family for giving me the time and space to see the project through (including weekends, holidays, and many meals). Special thanks to my sister, Jacqueline Arnot, Web site designer extraordinaire and able guide through the Internet.

Publisher's Acknowledgments

We're proud of this book; please register your comments through our IDG Books Worldwide Online Registration Form located at http://my2cents.dummies.com.

Some of the people who helped bring this book to market include the following:

Acquisitions, Development, and Editorial

Project Editor: Mary Goodwin

Acquisitions Editor: Mark Butler

Copy Editors: Christine Meloy Beck, Rowena Rappaport

Technical Editor: Nancy Schuster

Editorial Manager: Elaine Brush

Editorial Assistant: Paul Kuzmic

Production

Associate Project Coordinator: Karen York

Layout and Graphics: Lou Boudreau, Maridee V. Ennis, Angela F. Hunckler, Jane E. Martin, Anna Rohrer, Brent Savage

Special Graphics: Lou Boudreau, Drew R. Moore, Anna Rohrer

Proofreaders: Kelli Botta, Nancy Price, Rebecca Senninger, Janet M. Withers

Indexer: Sharon Hilgenberg

General and Administrative

IDG Books Worldwide, Inc.: John Kilcullen, CEO; Steven Berkowitz, President and Publisher

IDG Books Technology Publishing: Brenda McLaughlin, Senior Vice President and Group Publisher

Dummies Technology Press and Dummies Editorial: Diane Graves Steele, Vice President and Associate Publisher; Mary Bednarek, Acquisitions and Product Development Director; Kristin A. Cocks, Editorial Director

Dummies Trade Press: Kathleen A. Welton, Vice President and Publisher; Kevin Thornton, Acquisitions Manager; Maureen F. Kelly, Editorial Coordinator

IDG Books Production for Dummies Press: Beth Jenkins, Production Director; Cindy L. Phipps, Manager of Project Coordination, Production Proofreading, and Indexing; Kathie S. Schutte, Supervisor of Page Layout; Shelley Lea, Supervisor of Graphics and Design; Debbie J. Gates, Production Systems Specialist; Robert Springer, Supervisor of Proofreading; Debbie Stailey, Special Projects Coordinator; Tony Augsburger, Supervisor of Reprints and Bluelines; Leslie Popplewell, Media Archive Coordinator

Dummies Packaging and Book Design: Patti Crane, Packaging Specialist; Lance Kayser, Packaging Assistant; Kavish + Kavish, Cover Design

◆

The publisher would like to give special thanks to Patrick J. McGovern, without whom this book would not have been possible.

◆

Contents at a Glance

Cartoons at a Glance

By Rich Tennant

"FOUR-LETTER WORD FOR RESCUE! FOUR-LETTER WORD FOR RESCUE!"

page 71

"I'll start with 17 Across, and then I'll have the 37 Down, and bring me a bottle of the 61 Across..."

page 5

"Oh them? They create and sell crossword puzzles for a living."

page 131

"So you use a black marker to fill in the squares around your words? You're the same guy who cuts his jigsaw pieces to fit too, aren't you?"

page 105

"You've been so grumpy since you haven't been able to figure out that stupid six-letter word for malcontent!"

page 119

Fax: 978-546-7747 • *E-mail:* the5wave@tiac.net

Table of Contents

Part II: Sitting Down to a Sunday Puzzle 71

Part III: Exploring Non-Crossword Puzzles 105

Introduction

• •

*A*head of chess, bingo, checkers, and bridge, crossword puzzle solving is America's most popular brain food. In fact, baby boomers rank puzzles at the top of their daily routines, right alongside eating. It's no coincidence that 99.9 percent of newspapers in the U.S. carry a crossword in their pages.

In *101 Crossword Puzzles For Dummies,* Volume 1, you find a style of puzzle to suit every taste. (If you haven't figured out your style yet, the puzzles on the following pages may help you make up your mind.) Feel free to indulge yourself. This is one habit you don't have to feel guilty about: It's calorie-free and guaranteed to lower your blood pressure.

If something about those little square diagrams reminds you of the SAT, put that thought behind you once and for all. Don't think of puzzles as a test; no one is looking over your shoulder. And you don't have a time limit besides the one you set for yourself. Puzzles should relax, distract, and amuse. True, you may discover some new tidbit of information or recall some facts from the deepest reaches of your brain, but these are just side effects to the real focus of puzzles, which is fun.

If you are totally new to the world of puzzles, you should consider picking up a copy of my other book, *Crossword Puzzles For Dummies,* published by IDG Books Worldwide, Inc. *Crossword Puzzles For Dummies* is chock-full of solving tips and strategies to get you started.

Why a ...For Dummies Crossword Puzzle Book?

Yes, this book is different from those other puzzle books you see on the shelf or in the bins in the supermarket (you know, right next to the *National Enquirer*). *101 Crosswords Puzzles For Dummies,* Volume 1, delivers puzzles, puzzles, puzzles in a way that makes them easy and more fun to work:

- ✔ You get 101 puzzles that people actually like to work, including daily-size crosswords, Sunday-size crosswords, acrostics, diagramlesses, and cryptograms.

- ✔ The puzzles make use of today's most common *repeaters,* or words that frequently appear in crossword puzzles.

- ✔ The puzzles vary in theme and difficulty, but none of the puzzles is insurmountable. I provide solving tips and hints when I think you may appreciate a boost.

- ✔ The clues are easy to read, and the grid blocks allow you plenty of room to pencil in your answer.

- ✔ You have room in the margins and around the page to doodle with possible entries before you enter them in the grid.

✔ You always find the grid located close to the outside of the page, making it easy to write in your answers.

✔ Each puzzle has a number (and sometimes a name), making it easy for you to find the answers to your puzzle in Appendix A.

✔ I make the answer grids large enough so that you can actually read them. Go ahead and put away that magnifying glass.

How to Use This Book

I divide this book into five parts:

Part I: Having Fun with Daily Puzzles

Every puzzle in this part is approximately 15 x 15 squares, which should be the perfect size puzzle to conquer during your lunch break.

Part II: Sitting Down to a Sunday Puzzle

The puzzles in this part are generally 21 x 21 squares, which means that you may need to set aside some time to enjoy these puzzles. Most of the puzzles offer a theme to add to your solving pleasure.

Part III: Exploring Non-Crossword Puzzles

What does it take to be a "non-crossword" puzzle? In Part III, you find cryptograms, acrostics, and diagramless puzzles waiting for your amusement. Visit this part of the book for a little variety in your puzzle life.

Part IV: The Part of Tens

Part IV offers a quick guide to some of the best reference books and resources for puzzlers on the shelves (and on the Internet). You also get a quick tour of puzzles found primarily outside the United States.

Part V: Appendixes

You get to satisfy your curiosity in this part, which contains Appendix A, where you can find the answers to all the puzzles in the book. Appendix B offers a guiding hand to working the non-crossword puzzles you find in Part III.

Icons Used in This Book

I use icons periodically throughout this book to point out important tips and topics that I want you to know.

As in any game, puzzles have rules, both written and unwritten. Just to make sure that you're on your toes, this icon reminds you of these important rules.

Next to this icon you find advice and information that can make you a savvier solver.

Sometimes I offer hints on how to solve particular puzzles in the book. If you'd rather take a crack at the puzzle without my help, this icon steers you clear of any information that may spoil the challenge for you.

Part I
Having Fun with Daily Puzzles

The 5th Wave   By Rich Tennant

"I'll start with 17 Across, and then I'll have the 37 Down, and bring me a bottle of the 61 Across..."

Puzzle 1-1

Across

1 "Very funny!"
5 Ham-fisted one
10 Isn't capable of
14 College town on the Thames
15 "All kidding — . . ."
16 Spread in a tub
17 Spanish-American War figure
19 Pond floater: Lat.
20 Indulgence at the mall
21 Words before dare or whim
22 Told a fish story
23 Jealous to the max
27 Blanc or Brooks
29 Gidget portrayer Sandra
30 Okay grades
31 "What a pity!"
33 Science room, for short
35 Dramatic presentation
39 File-folder abbr.
40 Keep on hand
43 Part of CEO
44 *The Tortoise and the Hare* penner
46 Prohibition
47 Dick and Jane's dog
48 Flagmaker Betsy
51 Turkey topper
53 Numero —
54 Tiny place
59 Actor Baldwin
60 Southern constellation

61 Trattoria course
64 Prima donna
65 Sewing-kit item
68 "Your turn," in communications
69 Append
70 Whistle sound
71 Socially inept one
72 Trials
73 India, et al.

Down

1 Towel word
2 On
3 Timer, of old
4 Rage
5 Goal appropriate for this puzzle
6 "— live and breathe!"
7 *Black* — (Debra Winger film)
8 Like a paradise
9 Judge anew
10 Comes together
11 Tuckered out
12 Israeli desert region
13 Apple-polisher
18 Take seriously
24 Slippery swimmers
25 Straight up, at the bar
26 "For — a jolly . . ."
27 Peggy Wood played her on TV
28 Nobelist Wiesel
32 Stadium purchase
34 Float like a cork
36 Exile
37 Kind of sign
38 Prefix for plasm or derm
41 Sidewalk eatery
42 Was familiar with
45 Taro dish
49 Get short with
50 Long step
52 Erases, as a file
54 Wore
55 Cocktail garnish
56 — Brothers (Rinso makers)
57 Rounds of applause
58 Christine of "Running on Empty"
62 Captured, as in chess
63 "Them!", in the 1954 film
66 Small bed
67 Young- — (kids, colloquially)

Puzzle 1-2: Words Ending in "TION"

Sometimes two entries combine to make one answer — see 48 and 63 Across.

Across

1 Actress Shelly
5 Allege
10 Play divisions
14 Reputation
15 A Beatle
16 Stew
17 Wonder
19 Charles's sister
20 Governing body
21 Browned
23 Map abbr.
24 Angeli of Hollywood
25 Funny lady Gilda
29 Type of prize
31 " — Got a Secret"
34 Brainstorms, in Paris
35 Moe's friend
36 Pekoe, for one
37 Garret
38 Caprice
39 Letter opener
40 Silkworm
41 Grange
42 "Lorna — "
43 Word with mother
44 Celtic
45 Transgressed
46 Bakery worker
48 With 63 Across, rock group
49 Old-time deli
52 Fairytale boy
56 Witty
57 Type of gap
60 — about (approximately)
61 Useful
62 Therefore
63 See 48 Across
64 Spills the beans
65 Angry, with "off"

Down

1 Mauna —
2 Advantage
3 Alaska city
4 Smile
5 Moon feature
6 Liquid measure
7 Cuckoo bird
8 "— Rhythm"
9 Board game
10 Degrade

11 Regret
12 Prong
13 Luge
18 Interest measures
22 Breezy
25 Irked
26 Worship
27 Meaning
28 Seine
29 Stool sitter, perhaps
30 Theater sect.
32 Author Jules
33 Relieved
35 Fires
38 Union commander
39 Charles, to Elizabeth
41 Unicorn
42 Singer Ross
45 Wall St. terms
47 Hooded snake
48 Turtle's abode
49 Dramatic conflict
50 Leg bone
51 Head: Fr.
53 Printer's term
54 Ireland
55 Booth
58 Nothing
59 Tacit assent

Puzzle 1-3: Calling Earth

Across

1 Type of ticket
5 Rocker Sheryl
9 Pamphlet
14 Hodgepodge
15 — *Alone*
16 Type of student
17 Shakespeare's stage
20 Suit to a —
21 Press
22 High places
23 Dele's opposite
24 Coal containers
25 Bill of —
28 Dragged a guard to the ground?
29 Brotherly title
32 Fawcett's ex
33 Ripped up
34 Every fourth year
35 Longtime soap opera
38 Bobby Valentine's team
39 Drench
40 "— is everything!"
41 Sloppy pen
42 *The Bronx Zoo* author Sparky
43 Jonathan and Baldwin
44 Quayle and Steely
45 Picnic pests

46 Nanook of the north
49 Church choir member
50 "Son — gun!"
53 1968 film
56 Consumed
57 NH motto: "Live — or die"
58 Popular board game
59 Six-time U.S. Open winner
60 Type of letter
61 — *of the d'Urbervilles*

Down

1 Word with court
2 Model Macpherson
3 Adjutant
4 Diary
5 Feed the pet, make the bed, etc.
6 Isaac Asimov novel *I, —*
7 Portent
8 Wild companion
9 Cinematic sign-off
10 Simba's cries
11 Not pro
12 Center
13 Uno y dos
18 Famed mimic Rich
19 Called, as a cab
23 Persian rulers
24 Uncle Miltie
25 Wanders aimlessly
26 Map within a map
27 Los Angeles museum
28 *A Man Called —*
29 Savage
30 Where the deer and the antelopes play
31 Church nooks
33 Tim Allen sells them
34 Contained in 24 Across
36 "Uh . . . sure, OK!"
37 Tiny Tim's step
42 Carry on
43 "The Star Spangled Banner," e.g.
44 1982 Barry Levinson movie
45 Modify
46 Porthos' weapon
47 Belgrade resident
48 *Kiss Me —*
49 Hair style
50 Ron Howard role
51 *Daniel Boone* star Parker
52 Queries
54 "— the mark"
55 Linkletter

Puzzle 1-4: Playing Bridge

Across

1 Recedes
5 *Unsafe at Any Speed* author
10 "Zip- — -Doo-Dah"
14 Cry "uncle"!
15 Martini garnish
16 Jakarta's island
17 Incite
18 Tools for a quintet of gravediggers
20 Controversial ballplayer in 1996
22 In toto
23 WWII craft
24 Fleur-de- —
26 Cowboy's nickname
27 Actress Burke
29 "Senator, you're no Jack Kennedy" setting
34 Mashie, niblick, brassie, and spoon
38 Iced-tea add-in
39 Italian wine region
40 *The — of Kilimanjaro*
42 Encircle
43 Go to the land of Nod
45 Dr. Who's anatomical anomaly
47 Prepares the salad
49 Shipboard navigation system
50 Newsman Koppel
52 Neither's companion
53 Koppel's network
56 Paid a bounty to

61 Long overcoat
63 Ring centerpiece, often
65 Zone
66 "Garfield" pooch
67 — Dame
68 Big name in luxury hotels
69 Poetic time of day
70 "Slammin' Sammy"
71 Church part

Down

1 ERA part
2 Tree-trunk outgrowths
3 Archie Bunker-type
4 Pipe part
5 Basic
6 Actress MacGraw
7 Louganis feat
8 Newsreel segment
9 Took some time off
10 Not quite shut
11 Miami's county
12 Daredevil Knievel
13 — listening (radio format)
19 Computer-screen dot
21 Actor Baldwin
25 Public generator, perhaps
27 Helps with the dishes
28 "Life is Just — of Cherries"
30 Got the ball rolling
31 Mideast ruler
32 Cause for a lawsuit
33 They may be loose or tight
34 — Eddie Felson
35 European capital
36 Nomadic Native Americans
37 Black out
41 Blocked out
44 Lab dish
46 Viscount's superior
48 Coupes' big brothers
51 Exorcism target
53 Like a slightly-raised anchor
54 Borscht veggies
55 Make nuts
56 — *with a View*
57 Within: comb. form
58 Dam
59 Arabian Sea gulf
60 Spoil, with "upon"
62 Poet Teasdale
64 Hunter's lobby

Puzzle 1-5: Initial Offerings

Across

1 Perched upon
5 Flying-saucer maneuver
10 Bug repellent ingredient
14 Woman of tomorrow
15 On the ball
16 Willa Cather's *One of* —
17 Typographically-eccentric poet
19 Impulse
20 Christopher Robin's Dad
21 No-no
23 Playing marble
24 Defoe's Flanders
25 Baseball's Daulton
29 Hell's watchdog
33 They're sometimes abstract
34 Roy Rogers, née Leonard —
35 Pop- — (breakfast goodie)
36 Plant bane
37 Silver or Scout
38 Swedish rockers
39 Lincoln Memorial locale
40 Membership period, often
41 "Wozzeck" composer Berg
42 Billy Crystal offering
44 Lucille player
45 List-ending abbr.
46 Lobster-dinner need
47 "Eliminator" band
49 Rap-session leader
53 Skyrocket

54 Burglar
57 New Rochelle, NY college
58 Get the lead out?
59 — -European
60 A to B, i.e.
61 *60 Minutes* host Morley
62 Comic canine

Down

1 Get wrinkled, in a way
2 "— yellow ribbon . . ."
3 Richard Harris thriller
4 Horner's treat
5 *L.A. Law* hunk
6 In hock
7 Barn ornament
8 Diagnostic pic
9 Put back
10 It's never straight
11 Disneyland opener?
12 Descartes quote words
13 Lao- —
18 Some street performers
22 Eur. nation
24 Gangster Lansky
25 "— Duck"
26 Clio earners
27 Come together
28 Clunker
29 Pass over
30 Teacher
31 Far from pastoral
32 Comic Arnold
34 Like 1943 pennies
37 Nerve junctions
41 Monastery bigwig
43 "Who am — say?"
44 Squabble
46 Unconcerned
47 Sax man Sims
48 Author Grey
49 Tree growth
50 Glenn's state
51 "The Swedish Nightingale"
52 Space-flick character
53 Boom preceder, perhaps
55 Brady Bill opponents
56 Hostile force

Puzzle 1-6: Hiss!

Across

1 — *Jim* (Conrad novel)
5 Pinocchio, et al.
10 Egyptian cobras
14 *The African Queen* scriptwriter
15 Follow
16 Poke fun at
17 Hula costume
19 Ike Turner's ex
20 Flower part
21 Took the chair
22 "Star Spangled Banner" opening
23 Remove, as a derby
26 Lecherous looks
28 Happened, as a wish
32 Jay McInerney novel
35 Spoonbender Geller
36 Meddles, with "in"
38 Fashion look
39 Talk like Daffy
41 *Waiting for —*
43 2001, for example
44 Turkish title
46 *Robert's — of Order*
48 Chowed
49 Lay into
51 Has a share in
53 Actress MacDowell
55 Ball-game stopper
56 Rotisserie part
58 Still in the wrapper
60 Antonym to pathos
64 Samoan port, when doubled
65 Tuxedo wear
68 Molecule builder
69 Downy duck
70 *Born Free* lioness
71 Reading rooms
72 Hatchling homes
73 Type of court

Down

1 Falls behind
2 Fairytale baddie
3 Bring in, as crops
4 Notorious marquis
5 Guitarist Paul
6 Pen's partner
7 Sale-item tag
8 Countryish
9 Irish — (dog)
10 — General (cabinet member)
11 Beef entree
12 — colada
13 Collar insert
18 Slow-moving tree-dweller
24 Kermit, e.g.
25 Public uproar
27 Corn unit
28 Mea —
29 Opera solos
30 Long-running Broadway musical
31 "THIS —" (carton legend)
33 Give a keynote address
34 Social customs
37 Type of energy
40 Ghosts
42 Buddhist monastery
45 Give a hand to
47 Hogs' homes
50 Jute tree
52 Sporting-event opener
54 Spooky
56 Nail
57 — de foie gras
59 Ties the knot
61 Hawaiian city
62 Phrases of approximation
63 Sports-page figure
66 "Game, — , match"
67 12th-graders: abbr.

Puzzle 1-7

Across

1 Pre-schoolers
5 Witches' gathering
10 Sorrel
14 Came to rest
15 Old-womanish
16 Verge
17 Sly glance
18 Necessities
19 "Sore toe" disease
20 Syngman Rhee's nationality
22 Proclaims
24 Mil. mailing address
26 Iranian monetary unit
27 South Carolina's nickname
31 Medicinal mustard decoction
35 Century plants
36 Holyfield's work place
38 Gene make-up
39 Uttered
40 Aid or base, e.g.
41 Scold vociferously, with "into"
42 Trespass
43 Filmmaker Lucas's strange people
44 Kidney and soy, e.g.
45 Followed
47 Chosen one
49 Those others
51 "Elephant Boy" of '40s films
52 Instructed
56 Anneal

60 Heraldic border
61 Worship
63 Living room, in Mexico City
64 Eros, to the Romans
65 Claw
66 Poet's reference to Ireland
67 Termagants
68 Most favored, with "the"
69 What a politician takes

Down

1 Communicate verbally
2 Bread spread
3 Opera seating level
4 Poured
5 Unable to
6 Unit
7 Competed
8 Certain church official
9 Ignorant
10 Entertains in a grandiose manner
11 Aroma
12 Chills and fever
13 Catches
21 Mimics
23 Tibetan religious figure
25 Sober and dignified
27 Out of style
28 M. Delon
29 Pork or beef cuts, e.g.
30 Fragrant root
32 Tender medicine
33 Silly
34 Bottomland: Scot.
37 Certain road curves
40 Form a government
41 General Sherman's unusual name
43 Biblical charioteer
44 Nixon's friend Rebozo
46 Says
48 Hidden, as a talent
50 Chest decoration for a hero
52 Exchange for interest
53 Ms. Bombeck
54 Sabot
55 Bill's opponent, Bob
57 Remove a rind
58 Mr. Kazan, of Broadway
59 Verbalize zealously
62 Fabulous bird

Puzzle 1-8: Musical Hotshots

Across

1 Steal
5 Spare tire
9 ZIP code unit
14 Hare Krishna garb
15 Hot rock?
16 Mohawk River city
17 Sect's symbol
18 "Famous" name
19 Like a lion
20 "Anarchy in the U.K." group
23 Cord cutter
24 Fluffy feathers
25 Something to sling
28 Bed-and-breakfast
30 Finally
35 "— of robins in her hair"
37 "— go bragh!"
40 Lotion additive
41 He sang "Jessie's Girl"
44 Canine command
45 Chessman
46 Mistaken
47 Rocky Mountain capital
49 Law or saw ender
51 Take a shot at
52 Phillips University town
55 Doc bloc
57 "Rock and Roll, Hoochie Koo" singer
63 Dull
65 Pizza place
66 Long look
67 Dreadlocks wearer
68 Rule
69 Pisa pocket change
70 Thespian
71 Coaster
72 List extender

Down

1 Sandpaper feature
2 Ness, for one
3 Woodwind
4 The Brainy bunch
5 Blond
6 Nightingale accessory
7 Duck
8 Low man at La Scala
9 *Duck Soup* actress Margaret
10 Romance lang.
11 Lays down a hand
12 Wine cooler
13 Little bit
21 Splits
22 Nasal sound
25 Wetland
26 Join forces
27 Sticker
29 Rex's detective
31 Secluded place
32 On the ball
33 Cobbler, at times
34 — bear
36 Terrier type
38 Grande opening
39 Pitch-black
42 Bit of mischief
43 Manhattan Project scientist
48 Food for the gods
50 Made
53 Graven images
54 New Jersey skater
56 Special approach
57 Iron problem
58 Concerned with
59 Russo of the screen
60 Walk or trot
61 Old Testament book
62 Honest-to-goodness
63 Car-front cover
64 Varnish ingredient

Puzzle 1-9: Comparatively Speaking

Check for missing-word clues first.

Across

1 Agitates
6 Clock face
10 Recital performance
14 Lingo
15 Run in neutral
16 Support, with "up"
17 Absolutely reliable
19 Skin woe
20 Dress
21 Pioneer home material
23 Rooster's mate
24 New Jersey five
26 Rigid
28 Owns
31 Beef dish
33 Pedro's snooze
36 War deity
38 Lawman Wyatt
40 Fruit from palms
41 Fabled invention
44 Bury
45 Fr. battle site of WWII
46 Freelancer's encl.
47 Old German coins
49 Room additions
51 D.C. legislator
52 Send to Washington

54 — as a dog
56 NBC's Brokaw
58 — mater (brain cover)
60 Least damp
64 Region
66 The Bible, perennially
68 Post-Mardi Gras time
69 Opponent
70 Wonderland lass
71 Dove's dwelling
72 Halt
73 Sail holders

Down

1 Miniseries, perhaps
2 Word with turkey or dog
3 " — Rhythm"
4 Sculptor Auguste
5 Ogles
6 Excavate
7 False god
8 Apportion
9 Narrow projections
10 Baden-Baden, e.g.
11 Where winds blow?
12 Companionless
13 Shop sign
18 Certain volleyball player
22 A bit nasty
25 Dress lines
27 Ushers
28 Custom
29 Sports spot
30 Out-of-court deal
32 *Murder, She —*
34 Taunt
35 Colorado resort
37 Pittsburgh product
39 Hauls
42 Went awry
43 Real food, to a baby
48 Examines underwater fauna, e.g.
50 Blood-curdling sound
53 Council of — , 1845-63
55 *To — Mockingbird*
56 After-bath powder
57 Nabisco treat
59 In re
61 Yalies
62 Religious offshoot
63 " — bien, madame!"
65 Feasted
67 Gratuity

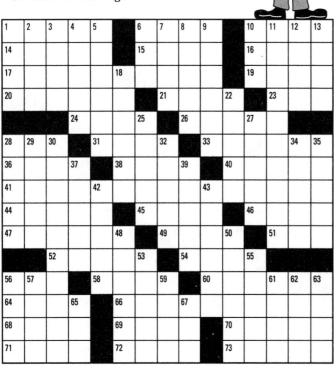

Puzzle 1-10: Getting Directions

Across

1 *Coming of Age in —*
6 Pie filling
11 NSO boss
14 Vocally
15 *Home —* (Macaulay Culkin film)
16 Card game
17 David Letterman segment
19 French law
20 TV's *Remington —*
21 "Sidewalks of New York" opening
23 Rod's partner
25 Blood, — and Tears
26 Baby seal
29 "Mack the Knife" singer Bobby
33 Whirlpool
34 Type of flu
37 Impressionist Pierre
39 Pivotal point
44 Madison Avenue come-on
45 Free-for-all
46 Prefix with well
49 Home-run great
51 "— it Be" (Beatles song)
52 Accumulate
54 Singer Martin
57 Choral compositions
61 Maine's — National Park
65 Explosive initials
66 Cut of steak
68 "— on a Grecian Urn"
69 Soda-bottle measure
70 Improve the text
71 Half a diam
72 Fill with glee
73 Farm towers

Down

1 H.S. exams
2 "Thanks — !"
3 Wear a long face
4 — Mongolia
5 Fred Astaire's sister
6 Chum
7 Nobelist Wiesel
8 — Nostra
9 Aardvark's meal
10 Hornets' homes
11 United
12 Gadget
13 Half, by law
18 Requirement

22 Veer
24 Arthur Godfrey regular Julius
26 — -man (arcade game)
27 Take advantage of
28 Bowler's target
30 Send, as to a specialist
31 Actress Bergman
32 Hide-hair connector
35 Give one's word
36 Society-page word
38 "How Dry —"
40 Aries symbol
41 Under the weather
42 Golf-ball holder
43 "Are we having fun — ?"
46 Max of cosmetics
47 Actress Plummer
48 Raved
50 Stitch line
53 Type of fur
55 Farm units
56 Wynonna Judd's mother
58 Slave away
59 "— boy!"
60 Editorial remark
62 Hamilton-Burr clash
63 — way, shape, or form
64 Uses a calculator
67 Smeltery input

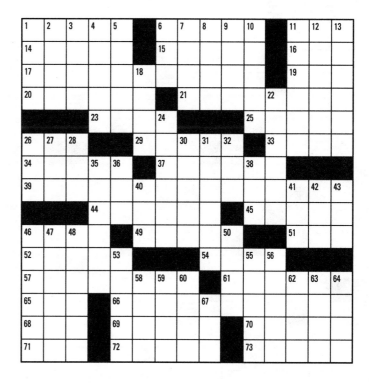

Puzzle 1-11: Says Who?

Across

1 Crucifix
5 George Bernard —
9 Spud
14 *East of Eden* heroine
15 Colombian city
16 Go along with
17 *The Odd Couple* playwright (full name)
19 Approaches
20 Majorca, to Pedro
21 Oath of yore
23 Last word from *Wayne's World*
24 Barbara Boxer, e.g.
27 Cartoon bubbles
29 Roger Moore role (full name)
33 "Monday Night Football" network
36 LEM seller?
37 Disreputable
38 Artist Chagall
40 "— mind!"
43 "The Man"
44 Chameleon's cousin
46 Soviet salt lake
48 Wind dir.
49 South American liberator (full name)
53 Goodbye, to Pierre
54 Rooms with a view?
58 GPA = 2.0, e.g.
60 Understands
62 — *of Two Cities*

63 Overalls material
65 Carrie Fisher's ex (full name)
68 Fragrance
69 *The — American*
70 Split
71 Grackles
72 Domesticated
73 Nice summers

Down

1 Punjab princesses
2 Overweight
3 Heavenly hunter
4 Series with J.R. Ewing
5 — -fi
6 Dr. Seuss' *Green Eggs and —*
7 Skin cream ingredient
8 Ad-lib
9 Stagecoach steeds
10 Iron or Bronze
11 Work at the United Nations
12 Architect Saarinen
13 Take five
18 Lingerie material
22 Lemon cooler
25 Arab sultanate
26 He finished with 4,256 hits
28 *Planet of the —*
30 Part of USNA
31 — *For All Seasons*
32 Chicago Cubs' Sandberg
33 After amo
34 Bucharest bucks
35 Early man
39 Klutz
41 Guitarist Clapton
42 Sitarist Shankar
45 Ambiguities
47 Turner and Lang
50 Spelling event
51 Assembly line production
52 Some do it at 65
55 *Glengarry Glen Ross* author David
56 *Home —*
57 E-mails
58 First mate
59 "— interesting!"
61 Norse narrative
64 "— Believer" (1966 Monkees hit)
66 Danube port
67 Sodium hydroxide

1	2	3	4		5	6	7	8		9	10	11	12	13
14					15					16				
17				18						19				
20						21		22				23		
24				25	26		27			28				
			29				30						31	32
33	34	35		36					37					
38			39		40		41	42		43				
44				45		46			47		48			
49				50	51					52				
		53					54				55	56	57	
58	59			60			61			62				
63			64			65		66	67					
68						69					70			
71						72					73			

Puzzle 1-12: Up in the Air

An abbreviation in a clue means an abbreviation in the entry.

Across

1 "Wynken, Blynken and —"
4 Minuteman's foe
11 Porkpie or Panama
14 N.Y.'s Madison, for one
15 4,840 square yards
16 Rio de —
17 Sorority since 1888
20 Packing a rod
21 Guinea pig's home
22 Diags.
23 Kind of artist
24 Victor's cry
26 Native American
27 Washington's men
30 Lady Bird follower
31 Kids' lids
32 NYC subway line
33 Bothered, colloquially
34 Grand finale?
35 Bill and —
36 Some radios: abbr
39 *The College Widow* author
40 Keep away from
41 Young man, in Oxford
42 Plains dweller
47 Red Square tomb occupant
48 McNally's partner
49 Islands music
50 Paul Desmond played it
51 Yodeler's perch
52 J. Carrol of filmdom
54 Surveyor's point
58 "If Winter comes, can Spring be far behind?" work
59 Ladies of Spain
60 Rode the bench
61 Actress Carrie
62 Like some toon turtles
63 1/6 fl. oz.

Down

1 Zero
2 Chesterfield, e.g.
3 Canned-veggie name
4 What away games are
5 It may be bitter
6 Poor grade
7 Talk-show talkers
8 45-degree arc
9 Yemeni, e.g.
10 Media mogul Turner
11 More moth-eaten
12 Eraser name
13 Warm and snug
18 Kind of stitch
19 Key of Beethoven's "Eroica"
24 Pretty quick
25 Shared grief
26 Marzipan ingredient
27 Apr. workhorse
28 Harborbound, in Alaska
29 Teem
35 Vandyke site
36 Most eccentric
37 Bull Run, to the Rebs
38 Campus protest gp.
39 In turmoil
40 Attaches, in a way
42 Support gp.
43 Rap's lack, usually
44 Admittance
45 Actress Dahl
46 Christmas-song title starter
51 Bide- —
52 Wall St. group
53 Web protocol letters
55 FDR successor
56 Singer's syllable
57 Carryall

Puzzle 1-13: Gumshoe

HINT

Another clue for 55 Down is "small measure."

Across

1 Singer Vaughn
6 Clever
10 Bars, in London
14 Swelling
15 Farm building
16 Virginia — (dance)
17 Inert gas
18 — Kadiddlehopper (Skelton alter ego)
19 Intestine: comb. form
20 Fictional detective
22 Action word
23 Cisterns
24 Stole
26 Preoccupied, with "out"
30 Main arteries
33 Tone
34 Minstrel
36 Ms. Kett
38 Indonesian Isle
39 Southpaw
40 Coup d' —
41 Betty of comics
42 Stake
43 Earp
44 Rejects
46 " — no place like home"
47 Guided on the dance floor

48 Greek peak
50 Inventor Elias
53 Settings for 20 Across
58 Abba of Israel
59 Petri dish gel
60 Robes for Caesar
62 Army org.
63 Crease: botany
64 Eared seal
65 — noire
66 Was aware
67 Low point

Down

1 Gender
2 Yemen's city
3 Descartes
4 Love god
5 Dartmouth town
6 Scarf
7 Brooks
8 Musical symbol
9 Recluse
10 Occupation for 20 Across
11 Belgian Congo's River
12 Favorite quaff of 20 Across
13 Oscar, for one
21 Bundle
25 Conjunction
26 Wound covering
27 Shirts
28 Thrown for — (surprised)
29 Obesity
30 Johnson of TV
31 Rose extract
32 Aver
34 Alexander and Hogan
35 Astern
37 Lwyrs.
39 Monument
43 Novelist Edith
45 Anent
46 Poet's monogram
48 Sioux Indian
49 Last item
50 Musician Alpert
51 Reed instrument
52 Voltage
54 Antisub weapon
55 Greek letter
56 Mild oath
57 Hindu wear
61 Neighbor of Isr.

Puzzle 1-14: Friends of Horatio Hornblower

Across

1 Devilfish
6 Not pro
10 Spreadsheet components
14 Keep from occurring
15 Haley costar of 1939
16 Tipped sword
17 Hornblower?
19 Word with primary or intensive
20 Fusses
21 AOL customer
22 Had the blahs
23 Albanian cash
24 Like mildew's milieu
26 Hornblower?
33 Held up
34 — -been
35 "All right!"
36 Ripken stats
37 Storrs sch.
39 Summer retreat
40 English-horn kin
41 Put down Bahia grass, perhaps
42 Eight-tracks
43 Hornblower?
47 Clay-pigeon launcher
48 Sports org.
49 Old-hat
52 Depict by drawing
54 Tom Jones' "— a Lady"
58 "Love Me Tonight" tune
59 Hornblower?
61 — even keel
62 Spherical opening?
63 Like the worm-catcher
64 Disqualify, Barris-style
65 Grasslands
66 Anglo-Saxon kingdom

Down

1 "I Remember —"
2 Enthusiastic
3 Agnew's plea, for short
4 Bow and neck
5 Many magazine pages, e.g.
6 Michener novel
7 Church area
8 Welles classic, with "The"
9 Spring collection org.
10 Interchangeable
11 Stone for some Scorpios
12 "— in the Money"
13 Pet-shop victuals
18 Membership charge

22 Qty.
23 Fish story
25 Part of AMA
26 Exert some influence
27 Heavenly hunter
28 Disturbing
29 Valerie Harper spinoff
30 Forest ruminant
31 Handles
32 Pulls a scam on
33 Forehead
37 Jimmy Carter's coll.
38 With nothing missing
42 Sorority letter
44 Hematite, e.g.
45 Superaggressive sorts
46 Yemeni capital
49 LA woe
50 Martinez of the Yankees
51 — *Called Horse*
53 Cookbook author Rombauer
54 Vichy and Baden-Baden
55 Towel word
56 Agatha's contemporary
57 River of Hades
59 Bacharach collaborator David
60 *Do the Right Thing* director

Puzzle 1-15: Do's and Don'ts

Across

1 Aleutian isle
5 Contented sound from kitty
9 Prudhoe Bay wear
14 Type of race
15 Sight from Sandusky
16 Wickerwork willow
17 1989 Spike Lee film
20 Precedes engine and shovel
21 Ooze
22 — Canals
23 Paul McCartney and Alec Guinness, e.g.
26 Where most people live
28 Protect the status quo
35 El Dorado's treasure
36 Marvel Comics' Lee
37 Prom transport
38 London district
40 Guiding principle
43 Zeno's home
44 Organic compound
45 Mystique
47 Final word
48 Manfred Mann hit
53 *High* —
54 Crossed off
55 1966 Monkees song "— Believer"
58 — fide
60 Citrus fruits
64 Animals hit
68 Boredom

69 Band of Pirates
70 Brainstorm
71 Roger Moore TV role, with "The"
72 Too much of a good thing
73 Maryland athlete

Down

1 Enhances
2 Jogger's gait
3 *Kiss Me* —
4 Horrified
5 — capita
6 Spoon bender Geller
7 Semis
8 Fix cold pizza
9 Meat and vegetable dish
10 Campfire fallout
11 *The Making of an American* author
12 Atlantic City game
13 Jason's ship
18 Kuwaiti rulers
19 TV host John
24 Campus mil. grp.
25 Appendectomy reminder
27 "Ready, willing, and —"
28 Prescribed medicine
29 Black Bears' home
30 "Not a chance!"
31 Work with dough
32 Lubricated
33 Correct
34 Sycophant
39 *The Good Earth* wife
41 Surfer's sobriquet
42 Gemsbok cousin
46 *Die Fledermaus* maid
49 *The* — (Tolkien novel)
50 Jim Morrison was one
51 Diamond division
52 Cry of accomplishment
55 Bad time for Caesar
56 — Lisa
57 Years, to Ovid
59 Indigo plant
61 Fashion
62 Lugged jug
63 First name in cereal?
65 Barrel of chianti
66 African antelope
67 Tom Seaver, once

Puzzle 1-16: Greetings

In a clue, the word "opener" means "prefix."

Across

1 Followed the leader
5 Rarely-seen bill
8 Bk. part
12 Mason title word
13 Like the Mojave
14 Serengeti group
15 Conspicuous?
17 Bill's foe
18 Prior to, poetically
19 Inland sea
20 Sunday celebration?
21 Name in a Neil Diamond hit
24 Within, in combinations
25 It may be bounding
27 Bluster
29 Scand. nation
30 Stegosaurus feature
33 Explorer Vasco da —
34 Feature?
36 Tot's seat?
41 Indomitable spirit
43 Froot Loops bird
44 Louisville Slugger wood
47 Tendon
49 Actress Lollobrigida
50 Butcher's cut
52 Recited the story

55 Appropriate hour?
57 Parcel
58 "Naughty, naughty!"
61 Ryan of *The Beverly Hillbillies*
62 Mel Brooks flick
64 VCR button
65 Gridiron great Graham
66 Autocrat
67 New Years, in Vietnam
68 Bk. of the Bible
69 1994 erupter

Down

1 Yen
2 Ace-high beater
3 Exceptional
4 — *Rosenkavalier*
5 Brief attempts
6 Compliant
7 Schiller's "— to Joy"
8 Inside job, for one
9 Scottish region?
10 "— Fideles"
11 Party, at times
13 Sixties do
14 Taro product
16 Crew implement
20 One of Herman's bandmates
22 Social opener
23 1983 French Open winner Yannick
25 Hwy. letters
26 Rope-a-dope inventor
28 Tijuana treat
31 They're sometimes coddled
32 Pilgrim's destination
35 Ike's ex
37 Brobdingnagian
38 Critical evaluation
39 Author Fleming
40 Cytoplasm stuff
42 Aardvark's morsel
44 Big name in trumpeting
45 Evening shindig
46 Gas choice?
48 Year-end ornament
51 Ball teams
53 Never, with "time"
54 Gore-— (fabric)
56 Lincoln Center building
59 Getz of jazz
60 Actress Sedgwick
62 Toots
63 Shi' —

Puzzle 1-17: Triads

Across

1 Approve
5 Light-switch position
8 Shells, for short
12 Somewhat: music
13 Delhi dress
14 Like a whistle
15 Everyday triad
18 Address
19 Vetch
20 — Luthor (Superman foe)
21 Ponce de —
23 Told a whopper
25 Distress call
28 Hog food
30 Prim and —
34 Sicilian peak
36 Bangladesh's continent
38 Pointless
39 Pie-throwing TV triad
42 — Haute, Ind.
43 Provoke, with "up"
44 San — (Riviera resort)
45 Tough time
47 Seth's father
49 Chaplin's son
50 Mrs. Kovacs
52 M.B.A. subj.
54 Spain's Costa del —

57 Type of stick
59 Hoodwinks
63 "Tom Dooley" singers
66 Confederacy's foe
67 Controversial orchard spray
68 Streamlet
69 Constricting snakes
70 Stick up
71 Double-reed instrument

Down

1 Makes a choice
2 Former Surgeon General C. Everett
3 Highest point
4 Alpine song
5 Acorn producer
6 Campus org.
7 End-of-term exam
8 — carte
9 Blackbird: var.
10 Filly's mother
11 Cameo stone
13 Rhodes —
14 Brit's greeting
16 Sorbets
17 Faucet problem
22 Snoops
24 Philanthropist, e.g.
25 Argument
26 Catchall category on a questionnaire
27 Dummy Mortimer
29 Michelangelo sculpture
31 Beeper calls
32 Hostile nation
33 Fix the lawn
35 — Grows in Brooklyn
37 Stage whisper
40 First of ten in bowling
41 John Deere machine
46 The — King
48 Dawn, to Keats
51 Actress Samantha
53 Explosive liquid, for short
54 Ticket remainder
55 "This can't be!"
56 Star Wars princess
58 Scandinavian capital
60 Nursery item
61 About 2.2 pounds
62 Fileted fish
64 Sends down for a 10-count
65 Restaurant bill

Puzzle 1-18: Who's Zoo in Fashion

Another clue for 15 Across is "Wing-like."

Across

1 Organ pedals
6 Greek-salad cheese
10 Super, to a Beatles fan
13 Darner's need
15 Controversial orchard spray
16 Immigrant's course: abbr.
17 What Fifi would wear to a '50s dance?
19 Tell — glance
20 Kind of toad or squirrel
21 Dorm-room hanging
23 Go bad
27 Flume floater
29 Earthy pigment
30 Signal sound
31 Actress Dern
33 Tear apart
34 Big name in porcelain figures
36 Sauce with fish
38 Microscopic-slide samples
40 On fire, in restaurant lingo
42 Speaks monotonously
44 Put a raised design on
46 Disfigure
48 Designer Perry
50 Emit coherent light
51 Lawn-neatening gadget
53 Baseball's Durocher
54 Stupefy with booze
55 Fill out a register
57 Inside, in combinations
59 Laugh syllable
60 What simians wear to weddings?
66 Where It. is
67 General Robert —
68 Catches sight of
69 Draft org.
70 Fly high
71 From Bhutan or Myanmar

Down

1 Oil-treatment letters
2 Even if
3 Rio de —
4 — XING
5 Like most bar munchies
6 Deceive
7 Actor Wallach
8 Field covering
9 — Detoo (Princess Leia's robot)
10 What snakes wear to fancy balls?
11 Behind, to Barnacle Bill
12 Bellowed
14 — *Rosenkavalier*
18 Actress Ward
22 Prepares eggs
23 Duplicate: abbr.
24 Elvers' folks
25 What mollusks wear to a beach party?
26 City officials
28 Steffi of tennis
31 *SNL* producer Michaels
32 Van Gogh's home, for a time
35 Gandhi successor in '91
37 Cap with a pompon
39 Broker's order
41 Exxon, once
43 More silky
45 Salon job
46 Fits together
47 Farewells
49 Actress Skye
52 Frosty coatings
54 *Blame It on the — Nova*
56 — contendere
58 Cover the gray
61 Teachers' org.
62 Increases
63 Sequel-to-a-sequel designation
64 Crumpets accompaniment
65 Nine-digit ID

Puzzle 1-19: Arthur Murray Studio

Across

1 Aid and —
5 Jelly
10 Make an aquatint
14 Israeli Premier of yore
15 Rock group, with "The"
16 Van Gogh's brother
17 Ballroom event
19 Air: comb. form
20 Settled a debt
21 Blew up
23 Distress signal
24 Matured
25 Hale
29 Song bird
31 "— King Cole . . ."
34 Utilize
35 Wharves
36 Shade of green
37 Sorry!
38 Mrs. Roosevelt and namesakes
39 Common catch-all
40 Prefix with way
41 Quoted
42 Allen or Martin
43 Actress Lupino
44 Keats ouput
45 Inclines
46 Knob
48 Actor Erwin

49 Most risque
52 — and feathered
56 "A — apple"
57 Recess event
60 In the — (healthy)
61 Fanon
62 Soccer great
63 Droops
64 Abated
65 Correct a text

Down

1 Cook's meas.
2 Teddy
3 Joyce's land
4 *The Parent —*
5 Director's word
6 Luges
7 *— Joey*
8 Wight, for one
9 War horses
10 Encampment
11 Ballroom event
12 Wax
13 *Boyz in the —*
18 Rhinal
22 Vessels
25 Ruth's daughter-in-law
26 Shun
27 Broadway event
28 Towel word
29 Connections
30 Peruse
32 Exit
33 Glens
35 Noodle
38 Fair exhibit
39 DDE's realm
41 Word with area
42 Eat noisily
45 Lingered
47 Sow's comments
48 Inscribed pillar
49 Sings, in a way
50 — Minor (peninsula)
51 African antelope
53 At the end of one's —
54 Supplemented, with "out"
55 Food shop
58 Neighbor of Neb.
59 Still

Puzzle 1-20: Ag-gies

Across

1 Polo
6 Vow
11 Rip-off
14 Lend — (listen)
15 Excoriate
16 "Alice" songwriter
17 Musician Isaac
18 *The —* (John Grisham novel)
19 Oahu necklaces
20 *Batman & Robin* actress Alicia
23 Honest —
24 Stat. for Randy Johnson
25 Genoa exports
27 Bon — (witty saying)
30 Actor Montand
33 Walk like Chester
34 1968 U.S. Open champ
36 Danube feeder
38 On the — (gratis)
41 Marvel Comics superhero
44 Bakery output
45 Beast of K2
46 Salamander cousins
47 Congers
49 Pro —
51 Vane dir.
52 Receptions
55 "It must have been something I — !"
57 Part of SASE
58 Tonto portrayer Jay
64 Oboe or clarinet
66 Utah national park
67 Swashbuckler Flynn
68 Deviate
69 Endo opposite
70 Saltpetre
71 Or — !
72 Ruby and Sandra
73 Run-down

Down

1 Neighbor of Conn.
2 Not pro
3 Angler's gear
4 Initial a tree
5 Ill-tempered
6 Rubs out
7 Came to a rest
8 Poi ingredients
9 Sunday songbook
10 *Exodus* actor Mineo
11 Bakery items
12 Court legal excuse
13 Basket case?

21 "Bolero" composer
22 Statesman Root
26 Dean Martin theme song
27 *Gunsmoke* Marshal Dillon
28 Govt. protection grp.
29 Faulkner's last novel
31 It makes you green
32 Show contempt
35 Fragrant compound
37 Mex. miss
39 Paramount features
40 Gaelic tongue
42 Man and others
43 Ravi Shankar instrument
48 Took control
50 Site of the Parthenon
52 Pete Sampras advantage
53 Shaquille of the Lakers
54 Pizza unit
56 Weird
59 Committee action
60 Adam's grandson
61 Art Deco illustrator
62 Michael Flatley's — *of the Dance*
63 Weaver's reed
65 Indigo, for one

Puzzle 1-21: Primrose Path

Across

1 Like some donuts
9 Colorful ring
15 Certain bacterium
16 Checked ID
17 It may be followed in Oz
19 Plopped down
20 Visualize
21 Actress Garson
22 — one's loins
23 Square
24 Sound broadcasts
27 Abets
28 Log opening?
31 *Miss America* author
32 Winemaking city
33 The yoke's on them
34 '80s TV drama
37 Building extensions
38 Just — (the slightest bit)
39 Muddle
40 Kind of serpent
41 Hand or foot
42 Man of the cloth
43 Assns.
44 — *But the Brave*
45 Himalayan land
46 WWII inflation-fighting org.
47 Welcome sign to a promoter
50 James Taylor cult flick

54 University board member
55 First to show
56 Idolizes
57 Diplomatic pacts

Down

1 Plunks down
2 Top-drawer
3 Mickey's creator
4 — Monte (food giant)
5 Rock-surface alterations
6 Shell crew
7 Declined
8 — *Rosenkavalier*
9 Authorize
10 Autumn workers
11 Goofed up
12 Musk, for one
13 Meadow
14 Total up
18 Set fire to
22 When tripled, a 1962 Elvis movie
24 Campfire residue
25 Helpful
26 Actress Reese
27 "Have —" (waiting room request)
28 Ooze out
29 Readies a banana
30 Map within a map
32 Entertainer
33 — but goodie
35 Geometry lines
36 Marine hanger-on
41 Suave
42 Warhol's genre
43 Houston gridder
44 Character actor Lloyd
45 Fast-food order
47 Editor's notation
48 American Beauty
49 Chooses
50 La-la lead-in
51 Hitched
52 Quilter's gathering
53 Relations

Puzzle 1-22: Doing the Wave

Across

1 Smooth
5 RBI, for example
9 Transported by Greyhound
14 Rawer than medium
15 — Alto, California
16 Contest mail-in
17 Suffix with teen
18 Ayatollah's land
19 In the know
20 World Series contenders
23 Before, poetically
24 — Moines
25 Supertanker's load
26 Tippler
27 "Home on the Range" animal
32 Stevie Wonder's "My Cherie —"
35 Germany's Graf von —
36 — *Master's Voice*
37 Front-page news
41 — Magnon man
42 Jimmy Carter's middle name
43 Chip away at
44 Like an old recording
47 Vessel that landed on Ararat
48 Ms. Farrow
49 Super — mo (TV playback)
50 Singer Garfunkel
53 Show-off, of sorts
58 Indian corn
59 Pro — (proportionately)
60 Baseball's Pete
61 Do some tailoring
62 Rocker Clapton
63 Poker payment
64 Flexible Flyers, e.g.
65 Mentally sound
66 Boot-camp meal

Down

1 Popular jelly
2 Beer
3 "Goodnight, —"
4 Swiss capital
5 Compact piano
6 What the Queen of Hearts took
7 "There oughta be —!"
8 Nobelist Morrison
9 Freshman's cap
10 Under the weather
11 Nova, e.g.
12 Goes wrong
13 Cover the gray
21 Love to death
22 Jotted down

26 — dried tomatoes
27 Silliness
28 Actress Patricia
29 "Say it ain't so!"
30 Like Hamelin's piper
31 Being, to Caesar
32 First-grade fundamentals
33 Artist Chagall
34 — about (approximately)
35 Former leader of 18 Across
38 Postgame rundown
39 Playwright Jones
40 Annoy
45 Astonished
46 Detroit's nine
47 — Lorraine (region of France)
49 — one's ways (obstinate)
50 Do penance
51 Takes a break
52 Oak and ash
53 Take a tumble
54 Word on lo-cal foods
55 Bauxite and galena
56 *Doctor Zhivago* heroine
57 Old London streetcar
58 Grad. degrees

Puzzle 1-23: Solid Solving

A question mark at the end of a clue may indicate a double meaning in the entry.

Across

1 Clever quote
5 Fuse
9 Razor brand
13 Europe's highest volcano
14 Tijuana
16 Like some champagne
17 Letter opener
18 Popular 3-D puzzle
20 Engine complement, sometimes
22 Regularly
25 Apropos of
26 — for tat
27 Sees eye to eye
30 Sites: abbr.
31 Robert Morse role
32 Snare sounds
37 Resting places of Khufu and others
40 Ceres or Pallas
41 Swinburne work
44 Throaty calls
47 Bloodhound, e.g.
49 Make the most of
50 E-5s
54 Moth—— (timeworn)
55 *SNL* characters
59 From 50 to 400 kilometers up, roughly
60 Judd Hirsch show

64 Ambler in literature
65 "— evil . . . "
66 First place
67 Search for
68 007's alma mater
69 Assents, in a way

Down

1 Proof ending
2 Western tribesman
3 — tizzy
4 Astronomical distance
5 Hart, Schaffner & —
6 Cabinet dept.
7 Land that's mostly Sahara Desert
8 Exerts elbow grease
9 Kindergarten tune starter
10 The Beach Boys' "Be — Your School"
11 Manuscript heading
12 Bikini blasts
15 Comedy bit
19 — -cone
21 Habituates
22 UN Day month
23 Pro
24 Bolt holder
28 Engrossed
29 Eye sore?
30 Leary letters
33 JFK stat
34 Pueblo people
35 Obote's deposer
36 Spruced up
38 — -been
39 Soap or water preceder
42 Wallace of *E.T.*
43 West ender?
44 Shrewd ones
45 Where castaways are often cast
46 Eloise's pet
48 Tie up
50 Call to the USCG
51 Economic stats
52 Giggle
53 Word with rap or scandal
56 Tilt to one side
57 First name of 18 Across's inventor
58 Many a millennium
61 Fuss and feathers
62 Marked a ballot
63 Election winners

Puzzle 1-24: A Day at the Beach

Across

1 — *Life Is It Anyway?*
6 Tournament rounds
11 Place for losers?
14 *The Age of Anxiety* author
15 Frankie of "Sunny Side of the Street"
16 Western moniker
17 Resist
19 From — Z
20 Clinton's canal
21 Orrin Hatch, for one
23 Withdraws, like a snail
28 In a high-fiving mood
29 Fertilizer ingredient
30 Spares
31 Vikki and John Dickson
32 *Little Red Book* writer
35 Scrambled alternative
36 Chief Justice, 1836-64
37 Dance spot, perhaps
38 Nancy Drew's beau
39 Scum locales
40 Canal sight
41 Animated flick of 1995
42 Independence-gainer of 1948
43 Saddam drew it
46 Weather-map line
47 Give the boot to
48 Russian fighter
49 Causing a disturbance
55 Fuss
56 Make up
57 *One Day at —*
58 W.C. sign
59 Posts
60 Arc-lamp gas

Down

1 Is no longer
2 Crude quarters
3 Tribute in verse
4 Course length
5 They're in the dictionary
6 Winter hazard
7 Scarf down
8 DI's double
9 Diligence
10 Boils
11 Colleague of Safer and Bradley
12 Corolla component
13 Nerve-cell part
18 Female deer
22 — Lingus
23 Agree
24 "Thimble Theatre" name
25 Dog- — (shabby)
26 At great length
27 Buenos —
31 Last words of "Over the Rainbow"
32 Gibbs of *The Jeffersons*
33 Light-bulb gas
34 Upright
36 Stand
37 Massachusetts nickname
39 Some hats
40 Business, slangily
41 Clothing protector
42 Labored engine sound
43 Words to the audience
44 Connect to the Internet
45 Earth — (browns)
46 Shi'ite leader
50 — -*Tiki*
51 Ball State: abbr.
52 — ordinaire
53 Funny Philips
54 Cong. member

Puzzle 1-25: All-Inclusive

Across

1 Flimflam
5 Window adornment
10 Te- — (cigar brand)
13 Precincts
15 Prelude to a blessing, often
16 High-muck-a-muck
17 Toolbox items
19 *Fables in Slang* author
20 Chow down
21 Feedbag morsel
22 Defender Dershowitz
23 Comes in quantity, with "to"
27 Precook
29 Foolish one
30 Trouble
32 Puzzlemaster Hook
33 Narrow opening
34 Be artistic
37 Market
42 Make certain
43 Menlo Park middle name
45 Part man?
49 — up (complete successfully)
50 React to a sunburn
51 Hollywood industry, familiarly
54 Gallant ones
56 Do some circus work
57 Rug rat

59 Paramount workplace
60 Series mo.
61 Den item
66 Greek R
67 Grid Hall of Famer — "Crazy Legs" Hirsch
68 Couric of TV
69 "What in — Hill . . . ?"
70 "Lorna —"
71 "You — it!"

Down

1 Gal of song
2 — -Magnon
3 NRC predecessor
4 Atone
5 Prosecutors: abbr.
6 Reverberate
7 Like Jack Benny
8 Main trunk
9 Pop band — Lobos
10 King Arthur's destination
11 Where some planes refuel
12 Without pretense
14 Trumpeter, for one
18 Low blows, e.g.
22 Exemplar of honesty
23 Laughingstock
24 Wire measures
25 Leave unmentioned
26 Stable parents
28 Actress Perlman
31 BMW alternative
35 Owning lots of land
36 Marathoner's impediment
38 Marathoner's intake: abbr.
39 Petroleum distillates
40 Gaiety
41 Lasting introduction?
44 Kaline and Jolson
45 Mary and John Jacob
46 Three-step dance
47 Snare's neighbor
48 Have a bill
52 Fascist leader Balbo
53 Douglas Fairbanks role
55 Dryer loss, perhaps
58 1982 sci-fi film
61 Lettuce arrangement
62 Sight site
63 — standstill
64 Golfer Davis Love —
65 One of Marge Schott's boys

Puzzle 1-26: Jewelry Store

HINT

"Ending " in a clue means "suffix" — for example, see 19 Across.

Across

1 Bowling-alley button
6 Pitt of screen
10 Mimics
14 *Remember the —*
15 Weak, as an excuse
16 *Same Time, — Year*
17 West Point student
18 Demonic
19 Ending with gang
20 Island gem, perhaps?
23 Pitcher's stat
24 Day- — (fluorescent)
25 Danish cheese
27 Bona —
30 Beige
33 What "i.e." stands for
34 Onassis, informally
35 Gin fizz flavor
37 Wee bit
38 Gem, to Moises Alou
44 Buddy
45 Use a swizzle stick
46 Western Indian
47 Former world org.
49 Screen at JFK
50 Will- — -wisp
51 Individuals
54 1/6 fl. oz.
56 — carte
57 Gem of a comedienne?
63 Latvia's capital
65 Abel's brother
66 Clarinetist Shaw
67 "Now I've — everything!"
68 Snarl
69 Midnight fridge visits
70 Once, once
71 Do in, as a dragon
72 Mr. Kefauver

Down

1 Kentucky Derby, for one
2 Khuzistan, formerly
3 "Cherry Pie" singer
4 Come out of hiding
5 Sum
6 Ran together, as dyes
7 Sitarist Shankar
8 Pennsylvania sect
9 Perry's aide
10 Ques. counterpart
11 Fizzled
12 Uses, as influence
13 — of Magellan
21 "— luck!"
22 Madonna role
26 Brother of Hoss
27 The — Four (The Beatles)
28 Tax-deferred acct.
29 Belittles
31 — *Well That Ends Well*
32 *Cape Fear* star
36 Work on a story
39 Chows down
40 Burst into flower
41 Hot under the collar
42 To the — degree
43 Poor grade
47 Not plentiful
48 More slippery
50 La Scala productions
52 Shavers' wounds
53 Slow one
55 Back up
58 One of Columbus's ships
59 Like octopus secretion
60 Keep — (persevere)
61 Carnival attraction
62 To a smaller degree
64 Picnic pest

Puzzle 1-27: Mixed Signals

Across

1 Take a — at
5 He hit 61 in '61
10 First name in vampires
14 Site of Scarlett fever?
15 School, to Pierre
16 First mate
17 Mixed signal
19 Author Grey
20 Set free
21 After Hebrews
22 French —
23 Porch, for Pericles
25 Give the creeps
28 Mixed signal
33 Choir members
34 Hall's partner
35 Pumpkin or pecan
36 Johnny Bench used one
37 Follow
38 Dry as dust
39 Spelling —
40 Not quite a swimmer
41 — stiff
42 Mixed signal
44 Stockpile
45 Shine's companion
46 Harrison Ford thriller *Air Force* —
47 Mushrooms, e.g.
50 Iron ore

55 On the briny
56 Mixed signal
58 Small gull
59 Firth of Clyde island
60 Pout
61 Son of Aphrodite
62 — -eater
63 Work units

Down

1 Betelgeuse, for one
2 *A — of Two Cities*
3 Soviet salt lake
4 — *in the Park*
5 Like Oscar's room
6 Summit
7 Crucifix
8 Type
9 Understand
10 Market
11 Dutch cheese
12 Referee who disqualified Mike Tyson
13 Iowa City rival
18 Grades
21 Montana and Namath
23 Planet observed by Galileo
24 Palm, for one
25 Rio dance
26 Tradesman
27 River critter
28 Wine tasting party dish
29 High-tech scalpel
30 *Faust,* for one
31 Buenos —
32 Exploits
37 Diner sign
38 "Everybody loves somebody —"
40 V-E Day setting
41 Clichéd
43 Liver and heart
46 Signs
47 Inevitable destiny
48 — friendly
49 Infamous fiddler
50 Oscar winner William
51 Jacob's twin
52 Dr. Frankenstein's assistant
53 Goon
54 Nice seasons
56 *2001* computer
57 El Dorado's treasure

Puzzle 1-28: Partners

Two clues can be directly related. For example, check out 49 and 65 Down.

Across

1 Watchdog gp.
6 Noted ranch
9 IHOP order
14 Censor
15 Marker
16 Pang
17 PARTNERS
20 Robin's class
21 Spin-doctor's concern
22 Omertà or bushido
23 WWW address
25 Composer Satie
27 PARTNERS
35 — Jima
36 *El — Presidente* (Asturias novel)
37 Fence crossing
38 Diamond protection
40 Located
42 Rotisserie part
43 Put out
45 — operandi
47 Shriver of tennis
48 PARTNERS
51 Sing "Rock-a-Bye Baby"
52 Swabbie's org.
53 "Begone!"
56 In motion
59 Bern's river
63 PARTNERS
66 Pressed for
67 Montreal street
68 Recession
69 Anne of *Archie Bunker's Place*
70 Ed.'s mail
71 First American saint

Down

1 "Fernando" band
2 Croat or Czech
3 "Le — Goriot"
4 Decennial count
5 *The Simpsons* storekeeper
6 *Schindler's List* star Neeson
7 — fide
8 Stallone flick
9 R.R. stop
10 Areas of impenetrability
11 Guthrie of "Alice's Restaurant"
12 Matriculated Ms.
13 *Kung Fu* regular — Luke
18 "Poseidon" sculptor Carl
19 *Mad Magazine* artist Dave
24 In medias —
26 Spring collection org.
27 Bandleader's command
28 Up to one's elbows
29 Like the Aesir
30 Talking-pig story
31 "— your life!"
32 Rod's co-star in *The Birds*
33 Inventor Howe
34 "— Call You Sweetheart"
39 Traffic-cop's command
41 Lake Superior city
44 Ostrich lookalike
46 "— your old man!"
49 First name of 65 Down
50 Powerless
53 Pond gunk
54 Chinese-calendar animal
55 Gymnast Korbut
57 Burden
58 Shelley compositions
60 Touch on
61 San —, Italy
62 Chris Berman's home
64 Crete's highest mountain
65 Ladd WWII film

Puzzle 1-29: And So to Bed

65 Axis predator
67 Advisor
68 — Boothe Luce
69 Madonna's "La — Bonita"
70 Ken-L-Ration rival
71 Nairobi's land
72 Let slip
73 Short time per.

Down

1 Nile biters?
2 Ruler exiled in '79
3 Grown-up leveret
4 Implant
5 Monaco's royal house
6 Corker
7 Applications
8 MASH figure
9 Choose
10 Hayley Armstrong player on *Melrose Place*
11 Fencer's weapon
12 Football coach Buddy
13 Wine center
18 Oklahoma tribesman
21 Bedroll alternative
25 Tony Musante series
26 Frisbee, e.g.
27 Fields
28 Abalone-shell liner
30 Extinct VCR format
31 Immeasurable depth
33 Comic Smirnoff
34 The end
36 Liner debuting in 1936
38 Wading bird
40 *Blame — Rio*
42 Sandberg of the Cubs
43 Of a body of water
48 Monte Rosa, for one
50 Fancy marbles
53 In the rules
55 Kind of bath
56 Tom's pal
57 Talented
58 Colorful horse
60 Get trounced
61 Slow interval
62 — *Well That . . .*
63 Run easily
64 Burger tycoon Ray
66 Afternoon social

Across

1 Net notable
5 Sad
9 La Scala offering
14 Bogus
15 Contrivance
16 English diarist
17 Precooked
19 Doctor
20 Pianist's purchase
22 "Crucifixion of St. Peter" painter
23 Edmond O'Brien film
24 Cosmetics brand
26 Decathlete O'Brien
29 Exile spot
32 Doolittle's attack site
35 Kuwait neighbor
37 Skater Thomas
39 Biscayne Bay city
41 "Peanuts" prop
44 Baseball Hall of Famer Max
45 Home of amahs and lamas
46 *Wake Me Up Before You —*
47 "I've never — purple cow . . . "
49 Barry Sadler, for one: abbr.
51 Workman's wheels
52 Dudley's beloved
54 Western treaty gp.
56 Wrong
59 1959 Doris Day film

Puzzle 1-30: What Was That Again?

Across

1 Girl in a Beatles title
5 Slammers' go-withs
9 Place for a battery
13 440-specialist's path
14 Rubbish
16 Repentant one
17 "What was that again?," geographically
19 Words before "boy" or "girl"
20 Program a smart card
21 Dollar alternative
23 Hill honcho
24 "What was that again?," cinematically
27 Recede
30 Erwin of early TV
31 No follower of Emily Post
32 Best friends
34 Poem of praise
36 Unconventional
37 "What was that again?," matrimonially
41 Resting place, of sorts
42 "Skittish" TV show?
43 — 'acte
44 Ruler of the Aesir
45 PC pioneer
47 Seaman
48 "What was that again?," musically
53 — -Aztecan
54 "Now it's clear!"
55 Go off the wall, perhaps
59 Sorority letters
61 "What was that again?" band
63 Pre-release version
64 Watts or Previn
65 Gad about
66 ". . . — I'm told"
67 Leering one
68 In debt

Down

1 Schoolboy of the diamond
2 "Terrible" handle?
3 One end of the Mohs scale
4 Earmark
5 Chain saw, for one
6 Son-gun linkup
7 Black key
8 Burst of fire
9 Calendar abbr.
10 Spate
11 Ended up using
12 Song syllables
15 Retreat
18 Troubles

22 "Here's mud in your eye!"
25 Autobahn auto
26 Head- — (completely)
27 Log opening?
28 Backbiter
29 Poppy family members
33 Protest
35 Ms. markers
36 Winter warmer
38 Tooth, in combinations
39 "Sit —!": Fonzie
40 Heavenly body
46 Nattering nag
48 Start to charge?
49 Poultry-package letters
50 See the old gang
51 Like a propellerhead
52 Introduction to surgery?
56 It's eaten in humiliation
57 Contain
58 Monopoly stack
60 — Luis, Brazil
62 Exist

Puzzle 1-31: Spring Training

Across

1 — of the D'Urbervilles
5 Labyrinth
9 It's a Wonderful Life director Frank
14 Yearn
15 Last year's Sr.
16 Expect
17 The — of the Cave Bear (Jean Auel)
18 City on the Truckee
19 Held up
20 Cut cowboy Rogers from the Missouri team?
23 Romance novelist Danielle
24 Moray
25 Nonprescription, for short
28 Brenda or Bart
32 Sixpence
34 — Ventura, Pet Detective
37 Modern day memo
39 "With the greatest of —"
40 Author Fleming dropped from California team?
44 Web —
45 Bicuspids, e.g.
46 Before tee?
47 Imprison
50 Escargot
52 — Are the Sunshine of My Life (Stevie Wonder)
53 Towel word
55 At — (on the loose)
59 Left comedian Costello off the roster in Missouri?

64 Teddy material
66 Border lake
67 "Blast!"
68 Actress Dunne
69 Garfield's lives
70 From — to Eternity
71 Kind of chest
72 Follows along
73 Bauxite and hematite

Down

1 America's Cup moves
2 Fanfare
3 Cry from Brandon De Wilde
4 Sight and smell, e.g.
5 Red planet
6 Actor Baldwin
7 New Mexico native American
8 Ham it up
9 European theosophy
10 MP's quarry
11 Rectory
12 — Tin Tin
13 Cleaned the plate
21 Modify
22 Not —
26 Trials and tribulations
27 Waldorf garnishment
29 Med. group
30 Rave companion
31 Cuts in small places
33 Prefix with natal
34 Drug analysis
35 Lorre role in The Maltese Falcon
36 Turned over to
38 Mortgage
41 Price
42 RR stop
43 Cause of Hidalgo heartburn
48 Black eye
49 "— the season to be jolly . . ."
51 Mariner's shout
54 — of a Woman
56 Not as common
57 Dirty look
58 — Park, Colorado
60 Sinatra's daughter
61 Puccini opus
62 Where Ali did his thing
63 Poor grades
64 Not my spelling
65 Jimi Hendrix's "— You Experienced?"

Puzzle 1-32: Conversation Pieces

Acoss

1 Ham's cousin
5 Seaweed
9 Resort
12 Outsize
13 "Here — the Sun" (Beatles song)
15 Pigsty fare
16 Tape format, of old
18 Zebulon, with a peak
19 Laugh at: obs.
20 Jacob's twin
21 March 15th, e.g.
22 Bering — (Alaska/Siberia separator)
24 Curve-drawing aid
26 Prince, perhaps
28 Looked at lasciviously
31 Applies with a cotton ball
34 Lion's digs
37 Bone up
38 Ostrich relative
39 Be tenacious
41 Actress Remick
42 George Burns prop
44 "Younger — Springtime"
45 People, to Pierre
46 Octagon's octet
48 Tibetan holy man
50 "Hooray!"
53 Ice cream, in Rome
57 Disseminated, as seed
59 — mater
61 Pilgrim John
62 Will- — -wisp
63 TV gadget of old
65 Social reformer Jacob
66 Sirloin, for one
67 Fairy-tale villain
68 Clairvoyant's skill
69 Art Deco master
70 Like Felix Unger

Down

1 Child and others
2 Erected
3 Moth
4 Prepares leftovers
5 Play part
6 Clinton's veep
7 Gather together
8 Sports-show summary
9 Calculating device
10 Slow —
11 Chimps, e.g.
14 Crossbones companion
15 Small piano
17 Kingston, for one
23 A — of Two Cities
25 Superlative ending
27 Pub missile
29 Biblical garden
30 Uses Clairol
31 Ten: prefix
32 Ugandan Idi
33 Driver's tool, of old
35 Suffix with fool
36 Iranian coin
39 — school (precollege institution)
40 Hose undoing
43 Skirt styles
45 Galleon
47 Boxes
49 — and potatoes
51 Fill with joy
52 Smoldering ash
54 Old saying
55 — -cotta
56 Beginning
57 Achy
58 '60s singer Redding
60 Like — out of hell
64 '50s presidential nickname

Puzzle 1-33: EN Words

HINT

In puzzles, you see architectural moldings like OGIVE or 28 Across.

Across

1 Argentinian on Broadway
6 — cadabra!
10 Icelandic folklore
14 "Go —!" (pep talk)
15 Christmas, in Calais
16 Brad
17 Stadium
18 Nov. 1918, event
20 Young lady, old style
22 Supervise
23 Meet again
25 Caresses
28 Molding
29 Fireplace nook
33 Guido's high note
34 Tip for a Sherlock
35 Atlantic or Pacific
36 "Ship of the desert"
38 Sullivan, et al.
40 Scarlett's Butler
41 — acid
42 Green pastures, perhaps
44 Sun. speech
45 Ryan of baseball
46 Genuine
47 Eagle's nest: var

48 Beatles' Rita
51 Units of electrical current
54 Lime trees
58 Burden
60 Imp
61 Part of HOMES
62 New Haven alumni
63 Actress Papas
64 Necessity
65 Jells
66 Analyze ore content

Down

1 Somewhat affected expletive
2 Cruz or Miles
3 Gossip paragraph
4 Pavarotti and Domingo
5 Astonish
6 Comparison by similarity
7 Slavic town
8 Take away
9 Vibrant
10 Dig in
11 Speaker's platform
12 Gaming cubes
13 Opposite of aweather
19 Elders
21 Study of env.
24 Irritating person, e.g.
25 Pie nut?
26 Texas Shrine
27 Sri Lankan language
30 Silly ones
31 Past time
32 Foyer
34 Laboratory replicators
37 Like cloisonné
39 All of a piece, e.g.
43 Jai —
46 Kind of shoe repair
47 Vipers
49 Places for chapeaux
50 Type of ink
51 Final word
52 Sink in mud
53 Balletic knee bend
55 Christmas and New Year times
56 Actress Foch
57 Weaver's shuttle
59 Twit, to a Brit

Puzzle 1-34

Across

1 Ornamental coating
7 Interfere
13 Chitchat
14 Past favorites
15 Ineffectual
16 Peter Serkin, e.g.
18 Emphasize
19 Actress Lamar
20 Very: Scot.
21 Lean–tos
22 Word with dish
23 Bargains
24 Afore
25 1962 Newman role
26 Proofreader's mark
27 Thought like Holmes
30 Greek play
32 Rail
33 Supreme Court wear
34 Relief pitchers, perhaps
37 Sequester
41 First month, to Juan
42 TV manufacturer
43 Kin to 42 Down
44 Troubles
45 — fixe (obsession)
47 Ticked off
48 El stop
49 Author Ambler
50 Messenger
52 Upset
54 Type of coat
55 Rise
56 Pressing need
57 Newscaster Stahl
58 Actor Segal

Down

1 Horse haven
2 Forewarned
3 Chaucer's format
4 Actor Burl
5 Noted T–man
6 — longa, vita brevis
7 Scooter
8 Leave out, in speech
9 June 6th
10 Racket
11 Type of suit
12 Undertook
13 Promoted
17 Prickly
19 Stashed away

22 Khartoum country
23 Breakfast order
25 Prefix with after
26 — San Lucas
28 CompuServe customers
29 Italian lake
30 Instant
31 Edwin Drood's betrothed
34 All Saints' Day, e.g.
35 Part of JFK
36 Backslide
38 Reverential
39 Actor Stamp
40 Get up and go
42 Kind of room, for short
45 Papas or Dunne
46 *The — Dozen*
47 More grounded
49 Daredevil Knievel
50 Make a hole
51 Therefore
53 Lt.'s training academy
54 Word with shot

Puzzle 1-35: St. Patrick's Day

Across

1 Wore a hole in the carpet
6 Likely
9 Counterfeit
14 Hot, hot, hot
15 Spoonbender Geller
16 "Workers of the world, —!"
17 Kind of acid
18 *Tour of Duty* setting
19 Actress Gallagher
20 March 17 theme
23 Corrida cheer
24 — *vu*
25 Bumbling sort
26 Give up
27 Commerce dept. stat.
28 Jack Lalanne's, e.g.
31 Enthusiasm
34 Site of Halcakala volcano
36 Attire
37 Operates perfectly
40 Cream ingredient
41 "— blue as blue can be"
42 "The Hoosier Poet"
43 Ozarks assent
44 Arthur of *The Golden Girls*
45 Type of door
47 Grooved on, in '60s slang
48 Treat for Little Jack Horner
49 — Dhabi (mideast port)
52 Canadian side of Niagara

56 Airline founded in 1927
57 Antiquated
58 Dickens' Heep
59 Ex–Mrs. Trump
60 Follow a bit too closely
61 Flat piece of paper?
62 Gas whose name comes from Greek for "strange"
63 Lumberjacking tool
64 SDI beam

Down

1 Picasso or Casals
2 Run — of (violate)
3 Mythical enchantress
4 Composer Satie
5 Some rings in '50s cereals
6 Pancake flour brand name
7 Vaclav Havel's capital
8 — Warner (media giant)
9 Unfair criticism
10 "— by land . . ."
11 Rock bookings
12 Mormon state
13 Byrd's title: abbr.
21 T-man
22 Ancient region on the Aegean
26 Pepsi rival
27 Resort cabin
28 Performer with a beachball
29 Reduce
30 "Be all that you can be" group
31 Vacationing
32 Word with model or playing
33 Plunge
35 Letters on a "Most Wanted" poster
36 It's most useful when it's cracked
38 Feudal lord
39 Stuffed to the limit
44 Chauffeur, of sorts
46 *The Murders in the — Morgue*
47 Alternative to Roto–Rooter
48 Showy flower
49 See 35 Down
50 Humdrum
51 Wedding helper
52 "— a nice day!"
53 — even keel
54 Fountain order
55 Vicinity
56 Snaps, perhaps

Puzzle 1-36: On the Threshold

Birds are popular in crosswords — see 41 Across.

Across

1 Oprah's bygone rival
5 Hosts, for short
8 "How — the little busy bee . . ."
12 Costa follower
13 A billion years
14 Duel tool
15 Utah city
16 Avon ad sound
18 Minnesota iron range
20 Forbidden
21 Elvis' specialty
23 Chart type
24 Dead hardware?
28 Town near Caen
31 Columnist Kupcinet
32 African tribesman
34 Snoop's device
35 Juror, supposedly
37 Earthquake shelters
39 *The Crying Game* star
41 Gull-like predator
42 Set up a bivouac
45 More Twilight Zone–y
49 Site for Whitman's lilacs
51 Kasparov's choice
52 Metric weight
53 Old French coin
54 Flock females
55 Indulges at a buffet
56 Surpass
57 Carry on

Down

1 Ball in a gym?
2 Take on
3 Adds frosting

4 *Algiers* star
5 Federal insurance program
6 Bill's partner
7 Uppity sort
8 Rubble
9 Friml production
10 Far: prefix
11 Maintained
17 Urban music
19 Former European capital
22 Narcs' units
24 Bowlful at a party
25 Galena, e.g.
26 Cold–weather gear
27 Consulted the dictionary
29 Outside a profession
30 Mrs. Saturn
33 Verifiable
36 Gets more ammo
38 More friendly
40 Bolger sang about her
42 Brink
43 Asta's mistress
44 Tense situation?
46 *The Music Man* setting
47 Tied
48 Whatever's left
50 Kanga's kid

Puzzle 1-37: Going Down!

When in doubt, look for a missing-word clue, which you can usually spot by the tell-tale dash.

Across

1 Singer McEntire
5 Totally opposite
10 Calamine lotion target
14 Woods choice
15 Not in the dark
16 City in Hawaii
17 Make it on one's own, or not
19 Netherlands town
20 Do a pizzeria chore
21 Use a recorder
23 James Dean–type
27 — Paolo
28 Laura Davie's org.
31 Powerful D.C. lobby
32 "The poison is time": Emerson
36 Ear opener?
37 Reviewer Judith
39 '50s TV "kid"
40 Nowhere near enough, with "a"
43 Add some zip
44 Trig ratios
45 Benz trailer?
46 Makes improvements to
48 Auction action
49 Produced
50 Bunch of thieves?
51 Scacchi of *Presumed Innocent*

53 Wall-to-wall alternative
57 Take out, perhaps
61 Awakening time, poetically
62 Lose one's heart?
66 Forget about
67 Bob
68 Son of Zeus
69 Goes out with
70 Dispatches
71 Collision consequence

Down

1 Kind of capital
2 Moran of *Happy Days*
3 "T" follower?
4 Istanbul, today
5 What's expected
6 Injection reactions, often
7 Word with blue
8 Like the Gobi
9 Negligent
10 Campaign output, often
11 Verdi opus
12 Lobster–pot component
13 — brew (do–it–yourself suds)
18 Poetic tribute
22 Special interest group, of sorts
24 Kind of owl or swallow
25 Gives off
26 Tongue — (scolding)
28 It may be in the soup
29 Jewish festival
30 Coconut—
33 Glacial ridge
34 Play part
35 Had in the bag?
37 Kind of block
38 Domingo, for one
41 Lockets, perhaps
42 George Eliot's *Adam* —
47 — out (destroys)
49 Story song
52 Catch some rays
53 "Famous" cookie man
54 "When in — . . ."
55 Part of HOMES
56 Beaufort scale category
58 Ran like heck
59 Square
60 Break
63 — Chaney
64 Chap
65 "— about time!"

Puzzle 1-38: Keeping Time

Across

1 Church tribunal
5 Iowa town
10 Fairy tale monster
14 Seabirds
15 Al and Tipper
16 Mates
17 Timekeeper
19 Palliate
20 Blue
21 Renters
23 After Nov.
26 Fool
27 Repair
28 Admonish
30 Hansoms
32 Nourished
35 Flamingos, e.g.
36 No — (plea)
37 Actress MacGraw
38 Skin soother
39 Elope
40 Town in France
41 Bo's number
42 Artery
43 Pallid
44 Tokyo, once
45 Singles
46 Ship's rear
47 "— Lisa"
49 T.V. network
50 Type of bread
51 Vacillates
56 H'way club
55 — Vista
56 Timekeepers
62 Dock
63 Le — (French port)
64 Irritate
65 Chilling: var.
66 Suffix with home
67 Ivy League college

Down

1 — judicata
2 Quartz, for one
3 Explosive: abbr.
4 Shade of blonde
5 Up at arms
6 Swinging things
7 An — and a leg
8 In order
9 Audience
10 Pacific, for one
11 Time keeper, with "clock"?
12 Musical term
13 Female sheep
18 Russian rulers
22 Cozy retreat
23 Forum
24 Expelled
25 Time keeper?
29 "— on a Grecian Urn"
30 Wagons
31 Emanation
33 Queen of mysteries
34 Quintuplet name
36 Menu
39 Kaisers, e.g.
40 Concorde, for short
42 The very best
43 Appraise
46 Dishonored
48 Eared seal
49 Director Frank
51 Use a VCR
52 Author Wiesel
53 Louver
57 First lady
58 Like a bone
59 Inlet
60 — in the Family
61 Wide foot

Puzzle 1-39: Tricky Twosomes

Across

1 Informative
6 Cleveland hoopster, briefly
9 Guns 'N' Roses guitarist
14 Glacier's leavings
15 American humorist George —
16 *The Outcasts of Poker Flat* author
17 LUMINARIES, BANDS
20 Lois's portrayer
21 Like some ulcers
22 Booth, for one
24 Superhero suffix
25 It's made bigger by pumping: abbr.
28 STALK, KISS
31 Capek classic
32 For no good reason
33 Fountain fill
34 Centers of activity
35 Bishop's topper
36 Patronize a runner
37 Passageway
38 To — (exactly)
39 — Lingus
40 Star in Aquila
41 3 R's org.
42 LIKELIHOOD, RESULTS
44 Misspeak
45 — Lobos ("La Bamba" band)
46 Father Time feature
47 *ER*, et al.

49 Org. cofounded by Helen Keller
52 FLESH, TUBERS
56 Dog-training site, perhaps
57 "— Beso"
58 Shells alternative
59 Without warmth
60 Religious sch.
61 Some mintmarks

Down

1 Tammany tiger creator
2 Romain de Tirtoff, to the art world
3 DON, SHRED
4 Constraint
5 Affirmation
6 Dinner duck
7 — up (makes sense)
8 Sunday duds
9 His or her clients frequently lie
10 Secular
11 20th-century avant-garde artist
12 Rel. title
13 "For — a jolly good . . ."
18 Ecstasy's opposite
19 Morceli's milieu
23 Yarn
25 EXPERTS, PRISONERS
26 Big name in geometry
27 Newsmen of old
28 Merciful
29 Priest, at times
30 Where gangplanks reside?
34 They're well-informed
36 Vigil spots
37 Pierce player
39 Do some decorating
40 "— of robins . . ."
42 Peripatetic Hazel
43 Flowering
47 Russian actress Anna
48 Sunday recess
50 Singer Lovich
51 Partakes of
52 Sgt. Preston, et al.
53 Lunch
54 Pfc.'s address
55 Copy

Puzzle 1-40: Rhyme Theme

Across

1 Hello, in Hilo
6 Spoonbill's cousin
11 — *Got A Secret*
14 Luxury car
15 Follow Daniel
16 Nancy Drew's boyfriend
17 Hollywood reporter of old
19 Hot drink, to Pierre
20 Before, to Burns
21 Garden tools
22 *Apocalypse Now* star Martin
24 Neighbor of Isr.
25 Ernesto's nickname
26 1,000 calories
27 Certain type of farmer
31 Cautious
34 — a pin
35 Genetic initials
36 Stereo: abbr.
37 Censure sound
39 Spiritual group
40 IRS rep.
41 — *Window* (Hitchcock thriller)
42 Baptisms, e.g.
43 "Chantilly Lace" singer
47 Stumbles
48 Pique
49 Bronze or Iron
52 Golfer Nick
53 — *Eagles*
55 — capita
56 Number of cards in a Roman deck
57 Featured act
60 Santa's helper
61 Doctrine
62 Quiz response
63 Vane dir.
64 Kind of board
65 Unleashed

Down

1 *Angela's* —
2 Suspicious
3 More weird
4 "I've — it up to here!"
5 Outcome of a coup d'etat
6 Necklace
7 Lasso
8 'Ooks, to 'Enry
9 Society page word
10 Shouting distance
11 Decipher
12 Passion
13 Land west of Nod

18 Laughter
23 Groovy as a cat
26 *The Parent* —
27 — Lanka
28 Calendario starter
29 Average grade
30 "Drat!"
31 Online conversation
32 Skedaddles
33 Heavenly experience?
37 Asks for alms
38 Chem. mixer
39 Paul McCartney, nowadays
41 Dueling thrust
42 Recite
44 Raised hand at Sotheby's?
45 Where the prodigal son ended up
46 Before a fall
49 Founded by Wozniak and Jobs
50 Gaggle members
51 Blew it
52 What Richard Kimble did
53 Type of Ranger
54 Aquarian prop
58 Haw's partner
59 72 at Augusta

Puzzle 1-41: In the Papers

Across

1 Daytime TV fare
6 "Loose — sink ships"
10 Monitors, with "keep"
14 Everglades bird
15 Step — ! (hurry)
16 Netman Lendl
17 Unaccompanied
18 Penalty
19 Flat-topped elevation
20 In-house publication
22 Composer Satie
23 Chart, with "out" ?
24 Chocolate name
26 Argentine grasslands
30 "— face!" (drill instructor's command)
32 Composer Stravinski
33 Dorothy's dog
35 Charged as a bill
39 Dressed to the —
41 Bossy's comment
42 Overweight
43 Grind, as teeth
44 Little troublemakers
46 M-G-M founder Marcus
47 Out of — (cross)
49 Fads
51 Moynihan's milieu
54 Get the picture

55 Math course
56 General — (onetime cabinet post)
63 Ramble
64 Cream-filled cookie
65 Hood of *The Little Rascals*
66 Arab port
67 Vaccine developer Jonas
68 Jump for joy
69 Departed
70 Model Macpherson
71 Pee Wee of Dodgers fame

Down

1 Actor Penn
2 Make goo-goo eyes at
3 "Pretty maids all in —"
4 Jots
5 "— by Starlight"
6 Exalted
7 "What's — for me?"
8 Type of cone
9 Caterer's food warmer
10 Third-grade lesson
11 Sidestep
12 Pesto herb
13 Cobra, e.g.
21 — *of Eden*
25 France's — Disneyland
26 B.B. sound
27 Once more, in Dog Patch
28 "— Lisa"
29 Hollywood type
30 Particles
31 Betty — (cartoon lady)
34 Leave unmentioned
36 Type of sign
37 Secondhand
38 Congregation's seat
40 Give it a —
45 Florist's unit
48 Calmness
50 "See Spot run" textbook
51 Camel's back breaker
52 Eat away at
53 *Separate Tables* star David
54 Feed the furnace
57 Face-to-face exam
58 Auction off
59 — -Coburg-Gotha (QE II family name)
60 John Wayne's — *Grit*
61 Right-angle bends
62 Word with interest

Puzzle 1-42

Across

1 Fishing and golf
7 Berry lead-in
11 Track and field distance
14 Matador
15 Como —? (How are you?)
16 Pie — mode
17 Like some numerals
18 Headliner
19 One of the whales
20 Profit, e.g.
21 Concerned
24 President after HST
25 The way, of Lao-tzu
26 Attorney General Janet
27 Certain choir members
29 Clear yellow gemstone
33 Kneeling one
37 Musical note
38 Roof overhang
39 Lumberman's tool
41 "Hip, hip, hooray!"
42 Waste allowance
43 Book for a Verdi opus
45 Delhi gowns
47 Actor Davis
48 Rip
50 Before, to Dickinson
51 Genetic printer, for short
54 Putting place
58 Egyptian goddess
59 Sound from the meadow
60 Stalk
61 Makes into law
64 Stout relative
65 Gardner of whodunits
66 Mexican painter Diego
67 — Moines
68 Namesakes of memorable
   impresario Hurok
69 Saved from harm

Down

1 All rise!
2 Studied closely, with "over"
3 Declaim
4 "Johnny —"
5 Angle or cycle lead-in
6 Weekend gatherings
7 Relax
8 Fall flowers
9 Gaze
10 Bill, to Chelsea
11 Endure
12 Opposite of aweather

13 Canceled debt
22 Written observations
23 Reassure
25 New Mexico art colony
28 Certain exams
30 Angelou or Frost
31 Dill, in the Bible
32 Zip
33 Fidos and Fluffies, e.g.
34 With avis, unusual thing
35 Ended
36 Diminutive
40 More sagacious
41 Canadian people of the First Nations
44 Audubon Society members
46 Feels
47 Author of *1984*
49 Companion to dome and turf
51 Kitchen tool
52 — Dame
53 President of Syria
54 Happy
55 Part to play
56 Ovine mothers
57 Iowa college town
62 Puppy bite
63 Actress Gardner

Puzzle 1-43: Spare Parts

Across

1 Sea stories
6 State
10 Mischief makers
14 Cheer up
15 Toll road
16 Secluded spot
17 In charge
19 *Illiad* locale
20 Till the turf
21 Political platform, perhaps
22 Stick
24 In a — (corner)
25 Mayberry moppet
26 Strolled
29 Missive from Maui, perhaps
33 Sorrow: poet.
34 Take a long look
35 Pahoa party
36 Gunslinger's dare
37 Sign of spring
38 Yen
39 Himalayan holy man
40 Earth tones
41 Madame de — (French writer)
42 Tastefulness
44 Marathon men
45 Cosmetic additive
46 Math term
47 Frequent fliers

50 Go one's way
51 Postal code
54 In a frenzy
55 On all sixes
58 Have a — (snack)
59 Open ocean
60 Plains Indian
61 Undo a dele
62 *Jane* —
63 Lively dance, to Henry VIII

Down

1 Right on!
2 Palo
3 Deserve
4 Utmost degree
5 More disreputable
6 Garden pest
7 Competes
8 Supplement, with "out"
9 Falls back
10 When the chips are down
11 Oliver's request
12 Type of judgment
13 Terrier from Scotland
18 Fairy godmother's prop
23 Morse code
24 Lose it
25 Leaks out
26 Confound
27 Punch line
28 "Put the — on Mame"
29 Webber's partner
30 Nimbi
31 Furious one
32 Combats of honor
34 Stephanie's mother
37 Never
41 Tunnel worker
43 Pub order
44 Wagnerian tetralogy, with "The"
46 Notre Dame neighbor
47 Short punches
48 Vent
49 Type of bag
50 Buzzing
51 Enthusiasm
52 Classic villain
53 ER procedure
56 Voice vote
57 Girls' grp.

Puzzle 1-44: Sound Comparison

Across

1 Distort
5 Kind of wave
10 Hurried
14 Love god, to Livia
15 Equally
16 Lover by the Hellespont
17 So long, in Livorno
18 An arm and a leg
19 Getting — years
20 Pickled
23 Parties
24 — estate
25 Strength: Lat.
28 "Enough!"
31 Last fellow in line
35 Blue–pencil
37 City in Siberia
39 Type of crystal
40 Thin, as *South Pacific*'s Honey Bun
43 Mountain maid
44 Pro — (proportionately)
45 Bawls
46 Trusted teacher
48 Touch
50 Napoleonic military leader
51 Long march
53 — *Pogo*
55 Very relaxed
61 Sign of remorse
62 Norse goddess of love
63 Uses a Lawn–Boy
65 The "A" in ABM
66 Irish patriot Robert
67 "No contest," e.g.
68 Worker protection agcy.
69 Procure, as money
70 Group in a roundup

Down

1 WWII servicewoman
2 In the center of
3 Lion's cry
4 Pleased with oneself
5 Daytime TV fare
6 Pelvis bones
7 Lowers, as the lights
8 "Allah — !" (Mideast cry)
9 Tenant
10 What a shawl covers
11 Magic's — & Teller
12 Actor Estrada
13 Get into, as a habit
21 Present–day
22 Friend of Pooh
25 Vitriol
26 "— you!" (challenger's words)
27 Ambulance sound
29 Actor Sharif
30 State of India
32 Hardly a genius
33 Hacienda material
34 Full of the latest dope
36 Italian café
38 Bruce Lee TV role
41 Scents
42 Make one's way through
47 — *Madness*
49 Hat size enlarger?
52 Destiny
54 Vitality
55 Magnifying glass
56 Pledge
57 Somewhat, for starters
58 Senate yeses
59 Filleted fish
60 Pitcher
61 Hoff's *The — of Pooh*
64 Heavy–hearted

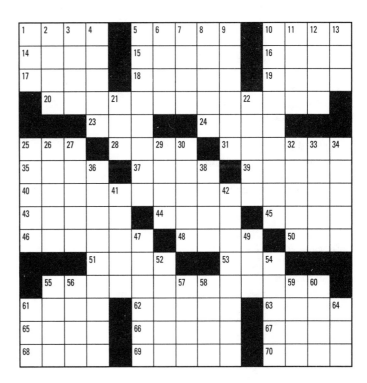

Puzzle 1-45: Petrified Forest

Across

1 Green shade
5 It may be saved
9 River inhabitant
14 Monster of folklore
15 Supply–sider's subj.
16 Terra —
17 Rocky Mountains city
20 Inter —
21 Reverence
22 Played to the snakes
26 Clodhopper
30 "Nude in the Sun" impressionist
31 Long–jawed fish
32 Actress McClanahan
33 Furious
34 Dennis Eckersley stat
35 "Requiem," for one
36 *Dateline NBC* cohost
39 God with a hammer
40 Blind part
41 Modern messages
43 Choice: abbr.
44 Search, as with radar
45 Ahmad or Phylicia
46 View
48 Zion National Park sights
49 — Lingus
50 Petroleum giant

51 Exemplar of genius
59 TV's DeGeneres
60 *Moonstruck* Oscar–winner
61 Brainstorm
62 — sine qua non (fundamental condition)
63 Pianist Dame Myra —
64 Wheedle

Down

1 Exemplar of patience
2 Past
3 Actress Joanne
4 Slithery swimmer
5 Antenna or tentacle
6 Unpleasantly pungent
7 Funny Imogene
8 Rock producer Brian
9 Looks at angrily
10 Edible mushroom
11 In–flight announcement, for short
12 Last letters, in London
13 Chinese philosophy
18 — *Omen II*
19 Half a famed comedy duo
22 Dernier —
23 Chocolate mecca
24 1921 Nobelist France
25 Dynamo part
26 Lifeboat support
27 Algonquian language
28 Thousand Island alternative
29 — Moines
31 Cartoonist Wilson
34 Snowball impact sound
35 "All — were the borogoves"
   ("Jabberwocky")
37 Guide
38 Pressure, loan shark–style
39 *Murder in the Cathedral* monogram
42 Mormon, briefly
44 Singer Easton
45 Indy entrants
47 "Land — alive!"
48 Reacts to onions
50 Aspirin
51 VCR button
52 Pay ending
53 Actor Gulager
54 Univ.
55 Spasm
56 Altar words
57 — legs (nautical steadiness)
58 Levy

Puzzle 1-46

Across

1 Crowning
5 Gather, with "up"
10 Lost
14 Author Jaffe
15 Baseball player Ryan
16 Outline
17 Mine entry
18 Swelling
19 A tense
20 Pool
22 Musical term
24 Word with split
25 "Come in!"
26 Wild pigs
29 — carte
30 Credit's antonym
34 Merit
35 Baden, for one
36 Loafers
37 Supplement, with "out"
38 Actress Weld
40 Alias: abbr.
41 Legal —
43 Type of ear
44 Something rare
45 Mollusk
46 Celebrity: abbr.
47 Oafs
48 Memento
50 Subscribe, with "into"

51 *Dynasty* role
53 Rubens, for one
57 Political group
58 Headgear, for Elizabeth II
60 Appeal
61 Dismounted
62 Sharpens
63 Egyptian goddess
64 Without, to Pierre
65 Growing out
66 Singer Johnny

Down

1 Russian sea
2 Fuss
3 Step — ! (hurry)
4 Paisley is one
5 Bergen's Mortimer
6 Kathie Lee's son
7 Pub order
8 Song of the '20s
9 Perform
10 Clothing
11 Balkan native
12 Put at one's —
13 Picnic pest
21 Navy officer: abbr.
23 A Roosevelt
25 Stretchy
26 Borscht ingredients
27 Proverbial bucket
28 Central space
29 Copy
31 Relative of bingo
32 Annoyed
33 Despots
35 Big — , Cal.
36 Writer Fleming
38 E-mail of yore
39 Chip's companion
42 Manages
44 Games in Australia in '98
46 Concept
47 Pool gadget
49 Flexible
50 Jaded
51 — breve (musical term)
52 Butcher's cut
53 Stew
54 Bergman role
55 After cinco
56 Corn beef —
57 — relief

Puzzle 1-47: You Name It

Across

1 — transit
6 Green Mountain
10 Courteous gesture
13 Iowa city
14 Buchholz of *The Magnificent Seven*
15 Triumphant cry
16 Indulge
18 Carlsbad Caverns dweller
19 Delivers the homily
20 Fall baby
22 Go out for some —
23 Pacific Islander
25 Not totally
29 Black lacquers
30 *Cheers* barmaid
31 Public uproar
32 Winning tic-tac-toe row
35 — 500 (race)
36 — off (appears)
37 Kerrigan feat
38 H.S. equivalency
39 — out (gets exhausted)
40 The latest fashion
41 Annual
43 Computing shortcuts
44 — of (more than)
46 Giovanni of opera
47 Lariat
48 Handel specialty
53 React to a tongue depressor, perhaps
54 Brawls
57 Rock's Brian
58 Prepares for publication
59 Not fulfilled
60 Bamm Bamm, to Barney
61 — *Man* (Estevez flick)
62 Billiards shot

Down

1 Freeway entrance
2 Cupid
3 Whitish in complexion
4 *To Live and Die* —
5 Working parents' concern
6 Physiques, informally
7 Fort — , Cal.
8 Fashion monogram
9 Outstanding
10 Early Sinatra fan
11 *A Rage to Live* author John
12 Valhalla VIP, to Wagner
14 Gardener, at times
17 IOU, of sorts

21 Actor Richardson
23 Stable dwellers
24 GI addresses
25 Hippie's "Understood!"
26 Cloud — (elated state)
27 Black Maria
28 "Have you — wool?"
29 Wired on caffeine, perhaps
31 They rush in
33 Wine: prefix
34 Early automaker Ransom E. —
36 Electrical wire
37 Circle part
39 Irishman on March 17, perhaps
40 Hissy fit
42 Dinner host's exhortation
43 Ancient mideast kingdom
44 Goads
45 Andre Watts' instrument
46 Prohibitionists
48 Aware of
49 Eugene O'Neill's daughter
50 PC components
51 Turner and DDE
52 Bone, in combinations
55 Keats work
56 Chill

Puzzle 1-48: Army Docs

Across

1 Christmas poem beginning
5 U, inverted
9 Wow
14 Comment from Chan
15 *Death on the —*
16 Patronizes Spago
17 First name in espionage
18 Way, way off
19 Until now
20 Army doc, perhaps
23 Once more
24 White wine and cassis
25 Peak in the Olympus Mountains
29 Without a contract, with "on"
31 Caesar salad morsel
33 Onetime strongman Amin
36 Grounded birds
38 It may involve a whoopee cushion
39 Army doc, perhaps
43 Cinders and Raines
44 Rover's repast
45 Previous to
46 Pre-show highlights
49 Elan
51 — speak (at this moment)
52 Farm worker?

54 Puts an end to
58 Army doc, perhaps
61 Utter confusion
64 — vac (battery brand)
65 Baltic port
66 Yemeni's neighbor
67 Neutral shade
68 Blockhead
69 Doc's O.K. Corral mate
70 Stock-exchange purchase
71 1991 has two

Down

1 Hav–a– — (cigar brand)
2 Fisherman's —, San Francisco
3 Up
4 Dry wines
5 Reviled one
6 Widespread
7 "Don't Sleep in the Subway" singer
8 Like Mighty Mouse
9 — 12 (TV show)
10 Battleship in the news on 9/2/45
11 Whatever
12 The Tappan — Bridge
13 Superlative suffix
21 Spread false charges against
22 Hockey legend Bobby
26 Condition
27 Fish–finding apparatus
28 Maxi's terminus
30 — –de–sac
32 At loggerheads with
33 "— Kick out of You"
34 Removes
35 Relative through marriage
37 — Na Na
40 Right of passage, e.g.
41 Long in the tooth
42 Be in a daze
47 British ruler, in India
48 Hammock sounds
50 Beehive, for one
53 Tinge
55 Descendant
56 "The Lone —" (Lindbergh)
57 Abbie's comic–strip partner
59 Touched down
60 Dame — Hess
61 Package finisher
62 Tan or Grant
63 Entreaty to Bo Peep

Puzzle 1-49: Separated at Birth

A Pope's name may include a numeral — see 59 Across.

Across

1 Architect van der Rohe
5 Abba —
9 Linguini, for one
14 Emulate Durer
15 Kinks hit
16 — Is Born
17 PETER
20 Actor Martin
21 Suffix with check
22 Change for a fin
23 Le Pew
25 Holler
27 Broadway hit circa 1964
30 Newspaperman Zuckerman
32 Brick carrier
36 Pop. author
38 James — Jones
40 Mary Tyler
41 PAUL
44 "Don't — me!"
45 The American Gigolo
46 RSVP enclosure
47 Latina singer
49 The King and I setting
51 New Jersey pro
52 Go through the mail
54 College study method
56 Length x width
59 5th century pontiff
61 Frank or Dweezil
65 MARY
68 Bert Parks, once
69 Goes bad
70 Type of bag
71 Silly ones
72 Prefix with while
73 Copies

Down

1 Queens team
2 Seven Year —
3 Yodeler's response
4 Black key, e.g.
5 "E" in BPOE
6 Australian invention
7 Edison's middle name
8 Type of habit
9 Word with off
10 List into
11 Ollie's partner
12 A — of Two Cities

13 Refuges
18 Gossip tidbit
19 Hang on to
24 Keats, e.g.
26 Gold brocade
27 The Silence of the —
28 Napoleon Solo's org.
29 Outspoken
31 Joyce Kilmer poem
33 Arthur Miller protagonist
34 Wipe out
35 Doctrine
37 Juniors
39 George and Ira Gershwin
42 City on the Truckee
43 At hand
48 A Guthrie
50 Minotaur's confinement
53 — Haute
55 Mediterranean island
56 Take down — (deflate)
57 Hoarfrost
58 Behold, to Brutus
60 Redolence
62 Watery sound
63 Tennis star Sampras
64 Parliamentary votes
66 Charge
67 Before DDE

Puzzle 1-50: All Smiles

Across

1 Saroyan character
5 Greek letter
9 Director Woody
14 Like 28 Across
15 *Blame — Rio* (1984 film)
16 Cacophony
17 Map abbr.
18 Defense org.
19 Kunta — (*Roots* role)
20 CB word
21 Politician, at times
23 Fix a text
25 Cordelia's father
26 — Antony
28 World's largest desert
33 Brilliantly–plumed parrot
36 Actor William
39 Shakespeare's river
40 Run — (go out of control)
41 Settle a debt
42 Annoying one
43 Housebroken
44 "— Bitsy Spider"
45 Shopper's binge
46 Bull sounds
48 Hang around
50 Secretary of State Janet
53 Hawke and Allen
57 Pirate's flag

62 Newspaper notice
63 Operatic offerings
64 Ye — shoppe
65 Over: Ger.
66 Kind of badge
67 Mediterranean and Adriatic
68 Weldoer's collaborator
69 Afrikaners
70 Humorist Bombeck
71 Ooze

Down

1 Socialite Brooke
2 Actor Christopher
3 Train stop, in Paris
4 Reveler
5 Caustic remark
6 Common catch–all
7 Wreck, as a car
8 Battery terminal
9 Turkey's capital
10 Pork purchase
11 "The Swedish Nightingale"
12 Villa d' — (Italian landmark)
13 At no time: poet.
22 Slapdash
24 Dad, to a hillbilly
27 Newsman Huntley
29 Cocktail times
30 State
31 Baseball's Pete
32 Feed the kitty
33 Gymnast's protectors
34 — *for All Seasons*
35 Crooner Perry
37 FedEx predecessor
38 Mantas
41 Step
45 Took a chair
47 Rendezvous
49 Mother —
51 Lariat loop
52 Lascivious looker
54 Slats' comic partner
55 Anne, to Princess Margaret
56 Bad throat
57 Doorway sidepiece
58 Nabisco cookie
59 Coins, in Rome
60 Bear's home
61 Dutch cheese

Puzzle 1-51

Across

1 Conscience prick
5 Type of party
9 Civil revolts
14 Egg-shaped
15 Escutcheon border
16 Invest
17 State of affairs
19 Parry
20 Sag
21 Dramatis personae, e.g.
23 Put one's — to the ground
24 Petition
26 M-G-M logo
27 Fit
29 Stuffy
33 Dardenelles, once
37 Yearn
38 Garfield's friend
39 Contract a debt
40 Favor
41 Minelli's daughter
42 Dominated
45 Forever
47 Butter substitute
48 Charged atom
49 One of a pair
51 Tibetan gazelle
54 Turns silver black
58 Texas columnist Molly —
60 The Ram
61 Caleb Carr subject
63 Hiatus
64 Productive vein
65 Covered promenade
66 Edible water plant
67 Lalapalooza
68 Catch sight of

Down

1 Volunteer police
2 St. Theresa's birthplace
3 Take citizenship
4 Mournful
5 Toper
6 Passe
7 Said with a lei
8 Recessive or dominant unit
9 Sometimes called Grim
10 Sacred

11 Music halls
12 Rotation
13 Pairs, dozens, cases, e.g.
18 Baldwin or MacIntosh
22 Aperture
25 — *Miserables*
28 Blurred eyesight
29 Pickle seasoning
30 Tree huggers?
31 Wingtip
32 You — Me
33 Place for toad or ace
34 Copy read
35 Snooker
36 Confess, with "up"
42 Preserves
43 Molder
44 Vegetable oil constituent
46 Thumps
49 Christmas or Casaba
50 Apart
52 "— of Old Smokey"
53 Appraise
54 Soft, gray mineral
55 Sandarac tree
56 Mature
57 Sundog
59 Clamp
62 Poetic word

Puzzle 1-52: School Days

Across

1 Confronts
6 Calf catcher
11 Impedance unit
14 Be mad about
15 Meryl Streep, to some
16 Boardroom VIP
17 It may require kid gloves
20 Considered
21 High, in combinations
22 Brownie, at times
24 Fort —, NJ
25 Give up
28 "I Fall to —"
30 St. Andrews shout
31 — -80 (old Radio Shack computer)
32 Part of USA
33 Sought–after objectives
35 1973 Glenda Jackson film
40 Dresses to the nines
41 Schwarzenegger, for one
43 "Pipe down!"
46 Bloke
47 Fridge decoration
49 Least remote
51 Mail, nowadays
52 Year–end abbr.
53 Entr' —

54 Stickler
56 Nothing unusual
62 Jersey's tail
63 Problem for Pauline
64 Anne of *Archie Bunker's Place*
65 Dime–novelist Buntline
66 Breaks one's back
67 March honoree, for short

Down

1 Streaking, for one
2 Humorist George
3 Sign of fearfulness, perhaps
4 Buffalo's lake
5 Drop out, officially
6 Rubber–plant sap
7 Scored
8 Ave. crossers
9 Small change
10 Sun or moon, e.g.
11 Spotted cat
12 Composer Berlioz
13 Artistic themes
18 *Lucky Jim* author Kingsley
19 Spree
22 Fed. watchdog
23 City north of Dayton
25 Goldbricks
26 Speed–skater Heiden
27 Spill the beans
29 Harvest haul
30 Dummy corporation, perhaps
33 1814 treaty site
34 Spilled the beans
36 More than suggest
37 So–so grades
38 Greg Norman's woe
39 Hook sidekick
42 And so on: abbr.
43 Attach, as a lining
44 Mythological haunter
45 Repugnance
47 Artist Chagall
48 Murphy's Laws, et al.
50 Foul caller
51 Stimulates, as an argument
54 "Punxsutawney —"
55 Plum–pudding ingredient
57 Choose
58 Classic car
59 Angular lead–in
60 Sp. lady
61 Chow down

Puzzle 1-53

Across

1 False alarm, so to speak
5 IRS employee
8 Expression of sorrow
12 Mideastern potentate
13 Wall St. wheeler–dealer
14 Fashion
15 Big rig
16 French king
17 Pair's piece
18 "Ala–Kazam!"
20 Piratic potable
22 Rich, raisen–studded cake
26 A Deadly Sin
29 Conk out
30 Incense
31 *Primal Fear* star
32 Every last crumb
33 Actress Swenson
34 Spoon–bender Geller
35 Numerical prefix
36 Broadway backer
37 Ethiopia's capital
40 *Some Like It Hot* costuming
41 Fish bunch
45 Shake in the grass?
47 Fun 'n' games
49 *The Neverending Story* author
50 Aid a crook
51 ". . . and seven years —"
52 Dogfight participants
53 Sagacious
54 Witticism
55 Nuisance

Down

1 Big stinger
2 Pre–Shavuoth period
3 Rickey flavoring
4 Low–flying aircraft?
5 Ersatz chocolate
6 Expert
7 Lady's maid
8 Zeal
9 Riant
10 Candle count
11 Prepared
19 Sailor
21 Wish otherwise
23 Extemporize
24 Desire
25 Powdery substance
26 Oaxaca water
27 Dweeb
28 Diner fixtures
32 Cast of characters
33 Filed up
35 Dream Team's logo
36 Popular network
38 Mad
39 *My Fair Lady* setting
42 Formerly
43 Praiseful poetry
44 For feat that
45 Gee's opposite
46 Where, to Caesar
48 Freudian concept

Puzzle 1-54: Heavily Seasoned

Across

1 Med. degree
4 Helicopter propeller
9 Allude
14 — room (play area)
15 Avoid
16 Florida city
17 "Honest" President
18 Extend a subscription
19 — rarebit
20 Candy flavoring
23 Guitarist — Paul
24 Howard and Isaac
25 Nerd
27 "None of the above" alternative
30 Subject of a will
33 *The — of the Mohicans*
36 Chief Norse god
38 Pelvic bones
39 Hospital sect.
40 Be quiet, musically
42 The whole — and caboodle
43 Carrying a gun
46 Butte
47 Poisonous snakes
48 Fish with a suction disk on its head
50 Tends to the sauce
52 "— Gay" (famous B-29)
54 — Bighorn (Custer defeat site)
58 Hockey great Bobby
60 WWI rifle
63 Exterminators' targets
65 Ryan or Tatum
66 "You're it!" game
67 '60s revolutionary Hoffman
68 Rollerblade, e.g.
69 Single
70 President Rutherford B. —
71 — Park, Colorado
72 Neither's companion

Down

1 Animals' stomachs
2 Credit's counterpart, to a bookkeeper
3 Part of an act
4 Lease again
5 Went beyond, as a mark
6 Sharp taste
7 River to the Baltic
8 Marry again
9 Deep-toned quality
10 Hockey-rink surface
11 Retreat positions
12 Celtic
13 College cheers

21 Horse's gait
22 Female ovine
26 O'Hare posting: abbr.
28 Wax-coated cheese
29 Chops finely, as potatoes
31 Excursion
32 Diner sign
33 Polygraph flunker
34 Plot size
35 WWII Eisenhower aide Kay —
37 Bird's — soup
41 Football fans' party site
44 Long time
45 Metallurgical waste products
47 — spumante (wine)
49 Mont Blanc, for one
51 Infantrymen's weapons
53 Came up
55 Grand — National Park
56 South American prairie
57 Lawn-neatening tool
58 Vividly colored fish
59 McEntire of country music
61 Fountain-pen fillers
62 Well-groomed
64 Outcome to tic-tac-toe

Puzzle 1-55: Calorie Counting

Across

1 Copies
5 Bridges
10 Ivan, for one
14 Horne
15 Weird
16 Fresh
17 Dieter's stable
19 Once more, in dog patch
20 Fixes the time
21 Develop
23 Robt. E. —
24 Ogle
25 Like a wet cat's back
29 Pare
31 Raincoat, for short
34 Live and —
35 Analyze a sentence
36 *Much — About Nothing*
37 Charged particles
38 MVP Yankee 1961–1962
39 Box
40 *El —* (Heston role)
41 Visit unexpectedly
42 Alabama city
43 English Isle
44 Alack's partner
45 Use a code word
46 Soft drink

48 Address, for short
49 Speechless
52 "Shake, — and roll"
56 Remit
57 Dieter's downfall
60 Understanding words
61 Down to —
62 Brief letter
63 Part of AMA
64 Shower
65 Snick's partner

Down

1 Pacino, and namesakes
2 Bosc, for one
3 Suffix with differ
4 Pouches
5 In place
6 By itself: Lat.
7 Onassis
8 Baseball need
9 Type of grape
10 Outline
11 Northeastern tree
12 Mine entry
13 Descartes
18 Actress Hayes
22 Belgian Congo's river
25 — Cooper (rock star)
26 Lubricate again
27 Holiday treats
28 24 a day: abbr.
29 Pierre's capital
30 — go bragh
32 Singer Edie
33 Mrs. Dithers and namesakes
35 Hemingway's nickname
38 Treacle
39 Wall St. watchdog
41 — Alto
42 Fitzgerald's middle name
45 Indifference
47 Word with days
48 Garbo
49 Continent
50 Tracy's girl
51 Barter
53 Large measures
54 Crazy as a —
55 Suffix with kitchen
58 Be human
59 Haw's partner

Puzzle 1-56: Recreational Real Estate

Across

1 Grad. degrees
4 Gymnast's concern
8 Current choices?
12 Clipper fliers
14 Eastern cuisine
15 It comes in tubs
16 Point of view
17 Part of 49 Across
19 Protest, of sorts
20 Behind
21 Some stadium surfaces
22 Part of 49 Across
26 Navigating
27 Met offerings
30 Volcanic residue
33 Like some *SNL* heads
36 Machete
37 Part of 49 Across
41 Late–night host
42 Christian music singer Patti
43 Actress Kirshner
44 007 foe
47 Charity
49 It has many properties
55 Ransom — Olds
57 Novelist Wister
58 Chou —
59 Part of 49 Across
62 1994 Nobel co–winner
63 Anna of *Nana*
64 Perry's creator
65 Attacked by bees
66 University founder Cornell
67 — Gold (pretzel brand)
68 Locane of *Melrose Place*

Down

1 Enthusiasm, plus
2 *Look Back In* —
3 Drool
4 PC data–exchange standard
5 *Butterfield 8* author
6 Less cooked
7 *The* — (1885 G&S opera)
8 Internet provider
9 Roll–call site
10 Art —
11 Dorm option
12 Tropical evergreen
13 Crescent–shaped bodies
18 Type of school
23 Light gas
24 Bunches
25 Neighbor of Wyo.

28 Half a court game?
29 Rickey need
30 Woody's son
31 Kind of pearl
32 Batter beater
34 Aldridge of the early stage
35 Panama or Erie
38 Sensei's spot
39 How some threats come across
40 Makes flexible
45 — about
46 Archer's supplier
48 One of Beethoven's 32
50 Prefix with dollars
51 — fours
52 It may have several cuts
53 Unpopular forecast word
54 Car–door nick
55 Choice word
56 Jump, Witt–style
60 Actress Merkel
61 Indicated a mistake

Puzzle 1-57: Big Brother

Across

1 — *Well That Ends Well*
5 Phase
10 Peacock Throne leader
14 Type of court
15 Redolence
16 Yorkshire river
17 BIG BROTHER
20 Screen Hercules surname, with 4 Down
21 Brit twits
22 Neither Rep. nor Dem.
23 Paris summers
25 *Dances With Wolves* cast members
27 Robert Shapiro passed it
30 Proofreader's "keep"
32 — roaring
33 Like Pegasus, technically
35 Site of Scarlett fever?
37 *Revenge of the —*
41 BIG BROTHER
44 Street corner cry of old
45 Actress Thompson
46 Ligurian Sea feeder
47 Model Carol
49 Mortgage, e.g.
51 Not —
52 Miss of etiquette fame
56 Oscar Madison, for one
58 "Thrilla in Manila" winner
59 Lug around

61 Fighting words
65 BIG BROTHER
68 Portent
69 Duck
70 Ersatz butter
71 Noted seamstress of yore
72 Aeries
73 "Trees," e.g.

Down

1 God of love
2 Ending for folk
3 *Tommy Boy* actor Rob
4 See 20 Across
5 Frankie Valli's voice, e.g.
6 Piece of parabola
7 Lawyer Roy
8 Modern memo
9 Tooth deposit
10 Pouch
11 Bandleader's phrase
12 Seattle's Key
13 "Moovers" and shakers
18 — *Make a Deal*
19 Inquiring
24 Navy elite
26 *Faust*, e.g.
27 1995 porcine fimstar
28 *Jeopardy!* host Trebek
29 Rave companion
31 Where the rubber meets the road
34 Played again
36 Peruvian highs
38 Silver screen cowboy Calhoun
39 Frank Herbert classic
40 Dick and Jane's dog
42 Parking attendants
43 Check–out counter rags
48 Bruin cross–town rival
50 — *Curtain*
52 Above captain
53 Davy Crockett's last stand
54 "Dressed to the —" (snazzy)
55 Cabin heater
57 Charlie Parker genre
60 *The Odyssey,* for one
62 *Mission: Impossible* theme creator Schifrin
63 Dirk of old
64 Ancient Dead Sea kingdom
66 The "I" in FDIC
67 Inebriated

Puzzle 1-58: Patriotic Folks

Across

1 Starring roles
6 Throat clearing sound
10 Responsibility
14 "Candle in the Wind" singer John
15 Nick's *The Thin Man* wife
16 Lack
17 By oneself
18 Geek
19 Kitchen suffix
20 Boston patriot
23 Rush
24 Prefix with corner
25 Loose pekoe container
27 — the line (obeys)
30 Pennsylvania city
33 — deco
34 Type of coat
35 Sir, in colonial India
38 Biblical prophet
40 *Clean and* — (Keaton film)
43 Fulfill
44 Red Cross founder Barton
46 Bikini top
47 — Abner
48 Authorizers
51 Dennis the Menace, e.g.
52 Memorial Stone
54 O'Hara's "— Joey"
56 Kuwaiti export
57 "Common Sense" pamphleteer
63 Fish story
65 Dueler's weopon
66 Hot under the collar
67 Line-— veto
68 Close at hand
69 Chou —
70 Cures, as leather
71 "A" in A.D.
72 Out of — (passe)

Down

1 Grazing sites
2 Scat queen Fitzgerald
3 Nuclear energy source
4 Pastries with coffee
5 Scornful look
6 — *Karenina*
7 Did some gardening
8 List of mistakes
9 Lunatics
10 Get a bill
11 1776 patriot
12 "— we meet again!"
13 Author Danielle
21 Thpeakth like thith
22 H.S. exams
26 Feathery wraps
27 Bath powder
28 Russian city
29 Leader of the Green Mountain Boys
31 Corp. VIP
32 Jewish scholar
36 "How sweet —!" (Gleason slogan)
37 Karate Kid's gear
39 Bodybuilders pump it
41 "Able was I — . . ."
42 Coarse files
45 Keep — (work tirelessly)
49 Parthenon goddess
50 Go back into business
51 Utterance of sorrow
52 Understood
53 Cowboy's rope
55 — ski (post slopes relaxation)
58 Ill-tempered
59 Aviation prefix
60 Bumpy, to a Cockney
61 *Hud* star Patricia
62 Adams, for one
64 Ambulance org.

Puzzle 1-59: Basic Grammar

Across

   1 Jewett's *Pearl of — Island*
   5 "— Fidelis"
  11 Deep–water food fish
  14 Harvest
  15 Marines' "— Fi"
  16 Lyric poem
  17 Idioms, for example
  19 Hillary Clinton, — Rodham
  20 Corrode
  21 Beretta, e.g.
  22 Swindle
  23 Place for "I do's"
  26 Crumb
  27 Pale pub potion
  28 "— me a story"
  29 Wk. night
  30 Riverboat
  33 Outgoing tide
  34 Blunders
  35 Sentence structure
  36 Plods
  38 Hobby
  39 Memorial speech
  40 Exercises, in a way
  41 Negative connector
  42 Trap
  43 Soothe
  44 Whining remark
  45 Type of pole?

  46 Word with pick
  47 Military installations
  48 Capitol Hill doctor
  50 Malayan isthmus
  51 Form of address
  52 Card game
  53 Q & A format
  58 Sea eagle
  59 Llama look–alike
  60 Anatomical lump
  61 Affirmative
  62 "Love — Number Nine"
  63 Teacher's note

Down

   1 Subterranean treasure
   2 *Oedipus —*
   3 2 Live Crew style
   4 Bed or point, e.g.
   5 Second banana: abbr.
   6 — Plaines
   7 Political refugees
   8 Speechifies garrulously
   9 Ark.'s next–door neighbor
  10 Found in the classifieds
  11 Squeezeboxes
  12 Music halls
  13 Judge
  18 Musical sensitivity
  22 Oblique
  23 Sharp ridges
  24 Albert or Vigee
  25 Calculator's output
  26 Not theirs
  27 Deep gulf
  29 Three–pip die
  31 Gamete connector
  32 Put forth effort
  34 Urged, with "on"
  35 Philosopher
  37 Electronic navigation device
  38 Fence support
  40 Pelota
  43 Transported, as an audience
  44 Solicitous
  47 Unit of computer data
  48 Reed for a loom
  49 Study intently, with "over"
  50 2.2 pounds
  51 Read swiftly
  53 Fly–fishing maneuver
  54 *The Name of the Rose* author
  55 Bill and —
  56 Fuss
  57 Guided

Puzzle 1-60: Uniformly Distributed

Across

1 Caught some Z's
6 Mood rings and Hula Hoops
10 Lawyer: abbr.
14 Home on the range?
15 Baldwin of *Prelude to a Kiss*
16 Mets ballpark
17 Arctic or Indian, e.g.
18 Show of hands, perhaps
19 Shipbuilding wood
20 Part I of a riddle
23 Recipe direction
24 Modernize, as a room
25 One's life, in 25 words or less
28 Short scissor cuts
30 Grind, as teeth
34 Make — meet
36 Pontiac model circa '64 pop hit
37 City that symbolizes middle America
38 Part II of the riddle
41 What comes from the heart
42 Ending with mater or pater
43 Word–mangler Berra
44 Bewildered
45 Up, in baseball
47 Vietnamese holiday
48 251, to Ovid
50 Radar blip
52 Answer to the riddle
59 Wrap for a rani
60 Hermes' mother
61 Please, in Potsdam
62 Photosynthesis "factory"
63 When Caesar is told "Beware
  the ides of March"
64 Composer Bruckner
65 Catch a glimpse of
66 Dates regularly
67 Broadway lights

Down

1 Pack away
2 President Walesa
3 Fencer's sword
4 Anjou and Barlett
5 Basic beliefs
6 #1 choice
7 Like a bump on —
8 Discourages, as attacks
9 Public spat
10 Where researchers do lots
  of looking up
11 "Take — Train"
12 Greenish blue
13 Chatters away
21 Inflatable raft
22 Gardening tool
25 Lebanese valley
26 Motionless
27 Playwright Clifford
29 "What's the —?"
31 Running rampant
32 — in for (begrudges)
33 Entertains at home
35 Harangue tediously
37 Buckingham, e.g.
39 Use a stencil
40 French satirist who created Gargantua
45 Eddie Rickenbacker, e.g.
46 Oedipus, by citizenship
49 Beans named for Peru's capital
51 Sheeplike
52 — of Wight
53 Opposite of ayes, in Edinburgh
54 Word before door or shoot
55 Location on the Web
56 "Sock — me!"
57 College founded by Henry VI
58 Washington 100: abbr.

Puzzle 1-61

Across

1 "O — mio . . ."
5 Challenged
10 Deflated feeling
14 First garden
15 Skirt syle
16 Charlie's girl
17 Care for
18 Crosswalk, with "crossing"
19 Seaver and namesakes
20 Makes secure
22 One of fifty
24 Reel's partner
25 Pertaining to the eyes
26 *Who's Afraid of Virginia Woolf* playwright
29 In a — (stuck)
30 Toga material
34 Needlefish
35 Bestseller, e.g.
36 — Thule
37 Wartime admn.
38 Papal district
40 — Alte (Adenauer)
41 Stoves
43 Hail, to Caesar
44 — out of shape (irked)
45 Mexican native
46 Wind dir.
47 Drives, as cattle

48 Stretch
50 Flightless bird
51 Type of piano
53 Currency
57 "Pretty maids all in —"
58 Sword
60 Italy's shape
61 Lopez's theme song
62 October stones
63 Pop. author
64 Call it — (quit)
65 Norman Vincent —
66 Actress Rowlands

Down

1 Bristle
2 Pindar's output
3 Camera part
4 Withstands
5 Shocked
6 Pub offerings
7 *Adam's* —
8 Charmed
9 Gave out, as cards
10 Belt, in New York state
11 Examine with "over"
12 Actress Paquin
13 Scornful reactions
21 Spawn
23 Bridal path
25 Exile
26 Greek marketplace
27 Bolivia's capital
28 Goose
29 Grande, for one
31 Sea duck
32 Correct, as a text
33 Bakery items
35 Towel word
36 Avail
38 Blame
39 First lady
42 Country cottage, perhaps
44 Popular toy
46 Grate
47 — pollol.
49 Fable man
50 Code man
51 Urge
52 She gets what she wants
53 Egg, e.g.
54 Tops
55 Thug
56 Italy's spurter
57 Prefix with gram
59 Black sheep's comment

Puzzle 1-62: Curious Crossbreeds

Across

1 Election day loser
8 Edith, to Archie
15 2.47 acres
16 Conduct business
17 Tomorrowland's town
18 Hispanics
19 Tree trunk
20 Tarnishes
22 Invigorates, with "up"
23 Perry's creator
25 "A — of Honey"
27 Out of style
29 Links score
30 Less normal
34 Like the hills
35 Kilmer of *The Saint*
37 Guernsey exclamation
39 Antique auto
40 Past
41 A Gabor
42 Leatherworker's tool
43 Failed amendment
44 Cornfield sound
45 Rented
46 Genetic material
47 Sib's nickname
48 Therefore
50 Lodge member
52 Tube
54 Saw
56 Corp. bigwigs
57 *Far — the Madding Crowd*
60 Glenn of *The Paper*
62 "If — a Hammer"
65 She played "Hot Lips"
67 Tenor Domingo
69 Acts the siren
70 — *States*
71 Data–input devices
72 Did a best man's job

Down

1 Moby's menacer
2 NBC's Jay
3 Snake–bird covering?
4 "Golden Rule" word
5 *Norma —*
6 Get out of bed
7 Verne sub captain
8 US–German currency unit?
9 Card–table comment
10 Bottom line
11 Bellyached
12 Ruin

13 At the summit of
14 Tracy's Trueheart
21 "Isn't — shame?"
24 Razed
26 After the fact
27 Prepare Benedict eggs
28 Pool problem
29 Eating–drinking utensil
31 Female–male garment
32 Like a creaky door, perhaps
33 Insult, kiddingly
36 Cathedral hail
38 *A League of Their —*
49 Was mentioned
51 Virgo preceder
53 Blanc's forte
55 Took measures
56 Yo-Yo's instrument
57 Criticism
58 Gig Young gig
59 Le Bourget alternative
61 Brief quarrel
63 *Song of the South* song syllables
64 *The Days and Nights of Molly —*
66 "— La La La Suzy"
68 One–time center

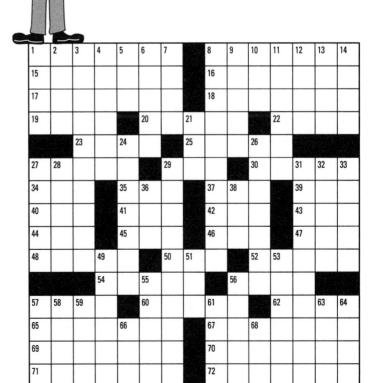

Puzzle 1-63: Hot Times

Across

1 Appear suddenly
6 Two before Leno
10 Geek
14 Seattle's Key, e.g.
15 Italian noble house
16 Melville novel
17 United States, in a way
19 Bully's weapon, in summer
20 — *Ranger*
21 Rock band — Pumpkins
23 Weapon in a silo: abbr.
25 Craggy peak
27 Command to Fido
28 Washington could not tell one
29 Canada's Grand —
30 Dagger of yore
32 — *off*
34 Baby powder
36 Modifies
38 Cause of the ocean's rise
43 Platypus, for one
44 Sunflower, once
46 Soak up
49 *The — of the Cat* (Al Stewart)
52 Humorous, in a sense
53 Mauna —
54 *The Flying* — (Sally Field)

56 RR stop
57 "I Can — For Miles" (Who song)
58 Decorated in a special way
61 Grande and Bravo
63 Stamp on a bill
64 Muscle relaxant
65 Ponderosa
69 Author Ferber
70 Skip the ceremony
71 Change for a fin
72 Actress Cannon
73 Scare off

Down

1 Dawber of *Mork and Mindy*
2 Bauxite or hematite
3 Helter–skelter
4 "Do — others . . ."
5 Creates a fresco
6 1977 Steely Dan hit
7 Nile nippers
8 Tiny building blocks
9 Downpayment for Robert Shapiro
10 Tidbit
11 Sends a letter without stamps
12 C & W singer Milsap
13 Eludes
18 Las Vegas gas
22 *Red — Rising* (Tom Clancy thriller)
23 Likely
24 Toot one's horn
26 Spectrum
31 Bronco quarterback
33 Sister of Osiris
35 Crooner Perry
37 *The Canterbury* —
39 Old MacDonald probably had these
40 Waylaid
41 Segment at 5:00 or 11:00
42 Actor Richard
45 Color, as an Easter egg
46 Syrian metropolis
47 Kingdom
48 Tribe of ancient Italy
50 Longfellow's bell town
51 Behaved like cats and dogs
55 Destitute
59 Pindar specialties
60 Funnyman Carvey
62 Gawk at
65 Author Amy
66 Aldoux Huxley's — *and Essence*
67 — *Rosenkavalier*

Puzzle 1-64: Get Physical

Across

1 Warsaw — of 1955
5 Procreate
10 Christiania, today
14 Connors opponent
15 *West Side —*
16 On the road
17 Beatles single featuring reversed tracks
18 Misbehave
19 Della, in *Touched By an Angel*
20 Dogpatch resident
22 Wishful container?
24 In a way
26 Oriental way
27 Overtime cause
28 10% of a sawbuck
29 Secluded spots
32 Choir platform
34 Irving Stone's — *for Life*
36 Food–label abbr.
37 ET's craft
38 Clams' midsections?
43 12–in. disks
44 Periodical, briefly
45 Hill residents
47 Ale complement
50 Slangy farewell
52 Before, to Burns
53 Southern constellation
54 Legal addendum?
56 Lower in dignity
58 Like bottoms?
62 *Quo —?*
63 Moon goddess
64 Man–year and foot–pound
66 Quickie–divorce town
67 Applications
68 Sizzling entree
69 Lascivious look
70 Saucy
71 Board game
72 The Grand Ole —

Down

1 Sunscreen
2 In addition
3 Violin part
4 Belief
5 Young men's gp.
6 Use acid, in a way
7 Sunday — meeting clothes
8 Explodes
9 Aggressive one
10 Hippocratic —
11 Desserts, generally
12 Glasgow gal
13 Stew morsel
21 TV host Reagan
23 Island of Greece
25 They may be filled in or filled out
30 Schiller's "— to Joy"
31 Fate
33 Island off Scotland
35 Communications leader
37 Drove onward
39 Church areas
40 Machine–gun syllable
41 Partially immersed
42 Kitchen gadget
46 Of touch or sight
47 Phone
48 Stir up
49 Marge Simpson voice Julie
50 Simple shelter
51 Gun the engine
55 *Green Eggs and Ham* writer
57 Thomas of TV
59 — *of Eden*
60 Layer
61 Have top billing
65 Shade of blue

Puzzle 1-65: Exit Lines

Across

1 Cass, for one
5 "Jingle Bells," perhaps
10 Do a tonsorial task
14 Burrows and Bigoda
15 Legend maker
16 Cure starter
17 "Goodbye to Love" singers
19 Civil disorder
20 "— was saying . . ."
21 Fabrications
22 Misses the cup
24 Cattail locale
26 Highway hellos
27 Patronized Sardi's
28 In a carefree manner
31 "— or When" (Dion hit)
34 Woo
35 A stooge
36 Maintained, as an opinion
37 Instruments for Clinton
38 Crazy as a —
39 Food grain
40 Puts on a long face
41 Smart money?
42 Expiate
44 Start of a daisy–plucker's phrase
45 Machine–gunners' spots
46 Word with snake
50 Indian dignitaries

52 *Cheers* regular
53 Mike–tester's word, often
54 Buckets
55 *Goodbye, Columbus* author
58 Germany's Helmut
59 Like a bucket of song
60 Out of port
61 Billie Holiday's "— Meeny Miney Mo"
62 The Guess Who's "— Eyes"
63 Jazzman Alpert

Down

1 Large parrot
2 Humble
3 Kind of pay or system
4 Cleopatra's killer
5 Incisor neighbor
6 Hit the big screen
7 Wishes one hadn't
8 Hockey immortal
9 Some rodeo participants
10 Dash of seltzer
11 *The Goodbye Girl* playwright
12 Hollywood figure
13 Absolute worst, with "the"
18 Overjoy
23 — laureate
25 Fat in the can?
26 Straightens out
28 George Foreman, for one
29 Spoils
30 Hankerings
31 Mountie's command
32 Police, slangily
33 "Goodbye Yellow Brick Road" singer
34 Guitar gadgets
37 Vulnerability
38 Eye maliciously
40 Fly–swatter material
41 Top dog
43 Between the lines, coloring book–wise
44 Where a vigil light burns
46 Old King and Nat "King"
47 *Northern Exposure* animal
48 PC key
49 Recovery program: abbr.
50 Sand–trap gadget
51 Sunburn soother
52 Sneaker maker
56 Scornful reply
57 Cheer

Part II
Sitting Down to a Sunday Puzzle

The 5th Wave   By Rich Tennant

"FOUR-LETTER WORD FOR RESCUE! FOUR-LETTER WORD FOR RESCUE!"

Puzzle 2-1: Words You Know

When you see the name Caesar in a clue, the entry is in Latin. For example, 88 Down, "Being, to Caesar," calls for a Latin entry.

Across

1 Apex
5 Mischievous children
9 Land measure
13 Bullfighter's cape
17 Bone film: hyph.
18 Tidy
19 Bend
20 Poetic "black"
21 Relaxed (with "at")
22 Great Lake
23 Astronaut Sally
24 Tubular light, sometimes
25 Egypt's colossus
27 Jeans material
29 Trap or snake leader
31 Tiny bites
33 Type size
34 Even the score

35 Men's undershirts
39 Hack, in the city
41 Fashion direction
45 Undivided
46 Mistake
48 Aeries
50 Miss West
51 News paragraph
53 Prongs
55 Sneaky
56 Confidential assistant
57 Rich veins
59 Turns ashen
61 Short, witty saying
63 Sped
65 Opponent
67 Soon: poet.
68 Farm machine
72 Goddess of crops

74 Embassy official
78 Divine
79 Dry wine, for example
81 Tehran money
83 High, neap or flood
84 In the manner of: Fr.
85 Pavarotti, e.g.
87 Malice
89 Common negative prefix
90 Companion to cotta or firma
92 Team of bulls
94 Seamstress' tool
96 Summer in France
98 Blemish
100 Other
101 Additional levy
104 ERA beneficiaries
106 Lone Star staters
110 Zone
111 Bosc or Anjou
113 Prince Charles' sport
115 Subject of Kilmer's poem
116 Danish author — Dinesen
117 Egress
118 — the Terrible
119 Holly genus
120 Glen
121 Spectacles part
122 — of our lives
123 French President

Down

1 Woodsman's tools
2 Follower of out or shoot
3 Notable former TV medical unit
4 Ogling
5 Rank amateur
6 Debussy's "La — "
7 Remitted
8 Let stand, as a teabag
9 Ethiopian or Sudanese
10 Most intense points
11 One of the primary colors
12 Make an effort
13 Mid-point
14 Give assistance
15 Game similar to billiards
16 Great Britain's Princess Royal
26 River in Egypt
28 Infesting insect
30 River islands: Brit.
32 Sunset follower
35 Smudge
36 Within
37 Necessity
38 Maritime electronic equipment
40 Capri or Emerald

42 Title for a Gulf prince
43 Nothing south of the border
44 Opine
47 Memento
49 Ilk
52 Compassion
54 Cut
56 Ten percenter
58 Perched
60 Gowns for Pakistan's Bhutto
62 Anger
64 Pay through the —
66 Bounds
68 Marlo Thomas sitcom, — *Girl!*
69 Actor's part
70 Winglike
71 Clinton's Attorney General
73 Bread portion
75 Chianti, e.g.
76 Aroma
77 Urges
80 Leader of a racing shell
82 Certain English cheeses
85 London farewell
86 What a newsperson does
88 Being, to Caesar
91 Capture again on film
93 — de plume: Fr.
95 Pertaining to the sixth
97 Eject
99 Lukewarm
101 Uttered
102 Heavenly Bear
103 Genuine
105 Brightening star
107 Woody's son
108 Depilatory cream
109 Risqué
112 English river in Devon
114 Troubadour's song

Puzzle 2-2: Vocabulary Building

If you're having some trouble with 59 Across, here's a little hint to get you started with the entry: The first letter in the entry is "R."

Across

1 Heredity element
5 Word on the Web
9 Coconut bearer
13 Alike
17 Employs
18 Inland Russian sea
19 Width times length
20 Jest
21 Tiff
22 Tennessee's nickname, with "State"
24 Biblical preposition
25 Cyclone
27 Drunkard
28 Kickbacks
30 Go astray
31 Illegally changed a check
33 French seasoning
34 Blackboard, formerly

37 Parted
39 Spanish hero
43 Misplace
44 Rental entertainment
45 Gesture of greeting
47 Tender
48 "— in the stilly night . . ." Moore
49 Jimson or tobacco, e.g.
50 Bumps and knocks, for instance
53 100 yrs.
54 Like Mediterranean winds in summer
56 Emerald or Capri
57 Hardy
59 14-line poems with a refrain
61 Offer a plan
63 Ms. Fleming of Hollywood
65 Sheltered, at sea
67 Twister
70 Assistance

71 Citizen of northern California
73 Wedge, as for a door
74 Peak
75 Little Kittens of nursery rhyme
77 Sign of a hit production
78 Fisherman's basket
80 Short-billed rail
81 Penn and Lennon
83 Artist's studio
85 Wall painting
86 Mournful
88 Molecules
89 Abbreviated endearment
90 Register person
94 Poisonous reptile
95 Tornado
99 Reflected sound
100 Obliged
103 Director Kazan
104 Leading lady
105 Medicinal plant
106 Fluency
107 Galahad and Churchill
108 Domesticated
109 Rents
110 British flophouse
111 Chimney refuse

Down

1 Short, sharp breeze
2 Discover
3 Low tide
4 Connoisseur
5 Taste; relish
6 Press, as jeans
7 Palm fiber
8 Evasive
9 Stroked, as a dog
10 "We — not amused"
11 Ogle
12 Colts' dam
13 Sudden offshore storms
14 Grandfather's daughter
15 Smidgen
16 Epic poetry
23 Opinions
26 Mine lode
29 Spelling event
31 Olympic skier Billy
32 Measure of fine hose
34 — gin fizz
35 Sleeping attic
36 Caucasian nymph
37 "Ich — ," (Prince Charles' oath of office)
38 Author John — Passos
40 Designing partner: hyph.

41 Annoyed
42 Say it isn't so
44 Jewish calendar additions
46 Plunder
49 Adjective for Chicago
51 Greek oil flask
52 Thunder and lightning accompaniment
55 Scion
56 — de Mujeres, Mexico
58 Follows Adm. or Ens.
60 One of the Siouans
62 Something else
63 Rug followers
64 Sign on for pay
66 Put in an envelope
68 Copperfield's wife
69 Multicolored gem
72 Victorian or Edwardian, e.g.
73 Dates
76 Wind from the sea
79 Wrinkled: obs.
80 Atmosphere in a cave
82 Breed of monkey
84 Troop camps
85 Soft-soled shoe, for short
87 Stick-on slogan
89 Park and Mr.
90 — la vie
91 Official records
92 Pillow cover
93 Evita, for Madonna
95 Tax; lien; Brit.
96 Mixture
97 De — of *Raging Bull*
98 Compass direction
101 Bon — ; witticism
102 Language spoke in southeast Asia

Puzzle 2-3: Expansion Teams

Across

1 Author of *The Other*
6 Start of Caesar's saying
11 Centers, as in seismology
15 Deface
18 Tree of the bush
20 Staff members, perhaps
21 Tiger club
22 Lode load
23 Dam drain
24 Choir group
25 Singer Celine
26 Filch: obs.
27 N.J. expansion team?
30 As well
31 Melodic passages
32 " — right with the world"
33 Fly, for one
34 Hydrocarbon suffix
37 Writer Rand
38 Feeds the piggy
40 Blender button
41 N.M. bench team?
46 Prefix with time
47 Roller-coaster fun
48 Fiddlers on the reef
49 Tropical fruit
52 "The Science Guy" on TV
53 Well, well, well!
54 Mother of Apollo
55 Something to chew on
56 Soda —
59 Mind finds
61 Letter embellishment
62 Salt Lake City athlete
63 " — you sleeping . . ."
64 Georgia expansion teammate?
67 '70s Cambodian leader
68 Bud holder
69 Dote on
70 RFD part
71 "Hey, Mac!"
72 Native Nebraskan
73 Confession material
74 Apiece
75 It can't be returned
77 Crosby band
79 "Dolly" composer
82 Neat: 2 wds
86 Clears
87 Oklahoma expansion team MVP?
89 "Giant" spread

91 Thelonious and son
92 Lennon's lady
93 Witt's milieu
94 One of the Great ones
95 Touch down
96 Beckett novel: 3 wds
100 — Francisco
101 Alabama expansion team?
107 Practice
108 Thereabouts: 2 wds
109 Grape place
110 Southeast Asian capital
111 "La —" (Debussy)
112 Consider
113 Take to task
114 Recent Surgeon General
115 Mr. and McMahon
116 Companion to ends
117 Enclosures, for short
118 Louis XIV, par example

Down

1 1/2 fluid oz.
2 Stethoscope sound
3 BYOB part
4 Last writes, perhaps
5 "Stille —" (Franz Gruber)
6 Trapped: 3 wds
7 Punctuation mark
8 Brief writers, briefly
9 Catty remark
10 Italian pronoun
11 String section
12 Bay windows
13 Rockies' — Field
14 Tabard and The Boar's Head
15 California expansion hot shots
16 Like 31 Across
17 Word with control
19 Easily endured
28 Pyramid builders
29 Transept transectors
33 Catamount
34 Show piece
35 Slangy dissent
36 Goof
38 You can get soaked here
39 Mass apparel
40 Split
42 World Wide Web connection
43 Artful
44 Dry fruit

45 Celeb. tournament
46 "Trois Gymnopedies" composer Erik
49 Jeopardy
50 Colt and Charger
51 Grunion kin
53 Kitchen emanations
54 "Merry Widow" composer
56 Rachel's husband
57 Milton's muse
58 Nev. expansion team?
59 They stand for something
60 Knight's address
61 Play starter
64 Zealots' last stand
65 Doors to ore
66 Corolla cousin
71 *The Royal Hunt of the Sun* setting
75 Make margin markings
76 "Le — d'or" (Rimsky Korsakov)
78 Ticket
79 Jane or Peter
80 Couples' craft

81 Hesitant sounds
82 Stoa style
83 Agnus — (*Missa Solemnis* section)
84 PC key
85 66, e.g.
87 Cpls. and CPO's
88 Yellowbellies
89 Rundown
90 Wiped out
91 Gathered together
95 Enticed
96 Riders of the rails
97 "— mio" (Italian aria)
98 On the whole
99 Nasty and insinuating
101 Big deal
102 Colleen
103 Willy, for one
104 Phone button
105 Infamous fiddler
106 Acapulco assent

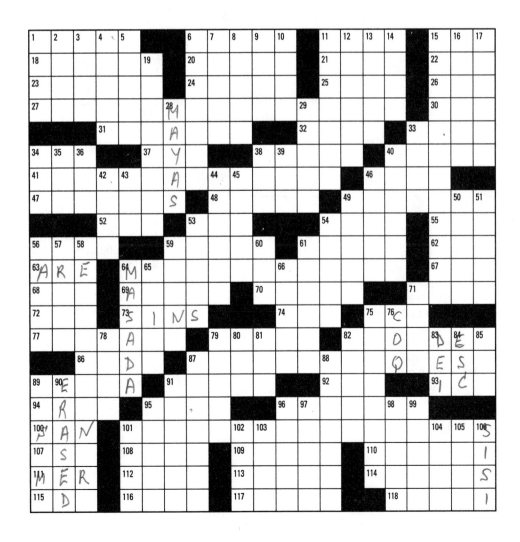

Puzzle 2-4: Gourmet Treats

Plural words in a clue mean a plural entry.

Across

1 Hog's cousin
6 Between shake and roll
12 Business letters
16 Positive electrode
17 Type of plate, perhaps
18 66, for one
20 Lowcal dessert order?
22 Courtyards, to Caesar
23 Quid pro quo item
24 Most unnerving
25 Residents
27 Prefix with while
29 "A long time — . . ."
30 Ivy Leaguer
32 Native: suffix
33 Like a red apple
35 Scooped up gently
37 Harry's wife
38 Sight: comb. form
41 Notorious trial
43 Scraped by, with "out"
45 *The Aspern* — (Henry James)
47 Writer MacDonald, et. al.
49 Allude, with "to"
52 "How sweet — !"
53 Truant's game
55 Arabian domain
57 Rainbow
58 Appetizer orders?
61 Job opp'y
62 "Babes in —"
64 Russian Union
65 Take a giant step
66 Actress Degeneres
67 Ness

70 Changed course
72 " — Misbehavin'"
74 A — one's mettle (challenge)
76 As a whole, with "en"
77 Hubbubs
79 Discontinued food coloring #2
81 Streets in Paris
83 Unit of work
84 Jinx
85 Author Deighton
86 Canal of note
90 Meal in Mykonos: var.
92 Rockrose resin
96 "All This — Heaven, Too"
97 Walking — (elated)
98 Entree orders?
101 Repeat sign: music
102 Things to rev
103 Grow accustomed to
104 Judge
105 Transferred, as land
106 Flower part

Down

1 Style
2 Sadat of Egypt
3 *Dead — Society*
4 Chemical suffix
5 Network: anat.
6 3/4, e.g.
7 Tennis great Arthur
8 "— means war!"
9 Old-time photos
10 Diary
11 Store, as grain
12 Seeing red
13 Strike the right —
14 Entree order?
15 Tasks
17 Counterfeits
19 Relaxes, with "up"
21 Type of tide
26 Brood of pheasants
28 Attempts
31 Church area
34 Neighbor of Leb.
35 BBC emcee
36 Phrase to a toddler
37 Lager
38 Religion, to Voltaire
39 Police beat
40 Side dish?
42 Gator's cousin
44 Kristofferson
46 Place for splints
48 Desert-like
50 Warehouses
51 Change, as a hairline

54 Nice wave
56 1555, to Caesar
58 Author of *Magic Mountain*
59 Emulated Updike
60 Producer Preminger
63 Welcome wear in Oahu
65 Landlord's document
68 Certain Fords
69 "Apres moi, —" (Louis XIV)
71 Dutch uncle
73 Pacific Island
75 Bridles, to Juan
77 Sample recordings
78 Pressed
80 Cleaned the slate
82 E pluribus —
84 Billiard shot
85 Intertwined
87 "The mouse — the clock . . ."
88 Prefix with mural
89 Classic car
91 Trig term
93 Sarcastic
94 Unit of force
95 Parisian matrons, for short
99 Hydrocarbon suffix
100 Vane direction

Puzzle 2-5: Separated at Birth

The answer to 61 Across is RAN.

Across

1 — and gown
4 Neptune's domain
7 Leather worker's tool
10 Trifles with
14 Abraham's mate
16 Killer whale
18 Set a — (corner)
20 Buck follower
21 Ogle
22 Told a whopper
23 Rocker Phil
24 Minnesota clinic
25 Separated at birth?
29 Actor Stoltz
30 Before PhD's
31 "— Miserables"
32 Fore opposite
35 Hydrocarbon suffix
36 Bill
37 Pop. author
39 Maple product
42 Norse prankster
44 Arista
45 Like an athlete
46 As to
47 Separated at birth
54 Vinegar container
55 Before, to Keats
56 Mollycoddle
57 — Lanka
60 Some att'ies
61 Kurosawa classic
62 Military address
63 "The Way"
64 "Pro —" (for the time being)
65 Under the weather
66 Elliot Ness, for short
67 Student's aid
68 Eithers' partners
69 Gas additive
71 Garden tool
72 Golden Horde member
74 Separated at birth?
81 British comic Eric
82 Believer: suffix
83 Liege commune
84 Pump
85 Islamic holiday
86 Goldfish family
88 Trio after A
89 Bartender's necessity

92 Actress Ryan
93 Neat as a —
94 "A mouse!"
95 Snoods
97 Separated at birth?
107 Mrs. Copperfield
108 Desert-like
109 "I cannot tell —"
110 Houston footballer
111 Ardor
112 Outfit for Bhutto
113 WWII division
114 Stiff upper lip
115 Salinger girl
116 Word before whiz
117 So far
118 Seasoning in St. Lo

Down

1 Orator Marcus Porcius
2 Mr. Khachaturian
3 "Gay —"
4 Comfort
5 "— Go Bragh"
6 Scored big
7 Bodybuilder Charles
8 Small bird
9 Colleen
10 Sec'ial help
11 Hours, to Juan
12 Duncan product
13 In a while
14 Quiet, at the library
15 Sesame St. regular
17 "Crazy Little Thing Called Love" singer
19 Mr. Vance, P.I.
26 Oriental demon
27 Chemist's workshop
28 Restroom sign
32 — In the Family
33 Pro
34 Ring decision
36 Company
37 Dale, starter
38 Ultimate degree
39 — attention (take notice)
40 Behind, as with a payment
41 Operatic Don, et al.
43 Business letters
44 Measures: abbr.
45 Parlor plant
46 "Big Blue"

g, as weapons
es
milieu
eels

tree
a hairline

Rex
tree
for example
ositions: abbr.
e World"

nd B&O, for short
— (vent)
row
Howard's —
78 Resistance unit
79 "— is me!"

80 Test result, for short
86 Colby's group
87 Karenina, et al.
88 Actor Kingsley
89 Jokingly
90 Corp. VIP
91 Community characteristic
93 Norman Vincent
94 Singer Gorme
96 Foul moods
97 Wood shaper
98 Fish eggs
99 Trolley
100 Type of race
101 Coins, in Rome
102 Palm
103 Where *ete*'s magnifique
104 Gin
105 Trompe l' —
106 Political org.

Puzzle 2-6: Whose Movie Is This?

Across

1 Mother of Invention
6 Shopper's need
10 Exchange, with "in"
15 RR depots
19 At right angles to the keel
20 Director Kazan
21 Make merry
22 London art gallery
23 1939 animated movie
26 Scholar's collar
27 Pipe part
28 Conceive, to Dickens
29 Norma —
30 Arthur C. Clark's *Rendezvous with* —
31 Sullivan and Asner
32 Opposite of wins
35 Put the check in the mail
36 African virus
39 1982 Meryl Streep movie

42 Bridge supports
45 Vintner's prefix
46 Also
47 Hoffman role in *Midnight Cowboy*
48 Breastbones
51 Mom's pal
52 "The William — Overture"
56 Burt Lancaster movie (1972)
58 Provide with weapons
59 Creepy
60 Rockers — Jam
61 James Caan movie (1970)
63 Furthest point
68 Ascot, for one
69 Stammering sounds
70 Reverberations
71 Anthony Hopkins movie
73 Soho slammers
75 Lacquer ingredient
76 Urge, with "on"
77 Mike Myers' movie

83 Colorado land feature
84 Prefix with where
85 Shampoo followers
86 "Full steam — !"
87 Turkish bigwig
88 Poe's *The Gold* —
89 Fetch
91 1973 animated movie
98 Battery terminal
99 Arthur Hailey novel
100 C2H6
101 Cool dessert, in Berlin
102 Major ending
103 Danson
105 Doling out
107 Fleur-de-lis
111 Lament
112 Arlo Guthrie movie (1969)
116 Land of the leprechauns
117 "Round up the — suspects"
118 Mirth
119 Where Ali defeated Foreman
120 — Scott decision
121 Buccaneer's home
122 Belgian river
123 Precedes sanctum or circle

Down

1 After zigs
2 Lie adjacent to
3 Edson Arantes de Nascimento
4 Desert or Beach
5 Brigitte's buddy
6 English city
7 Mozart's "— Pastore"
8 Cord fibers
9 Dennis Rodman feature
10 La-la lead in
11 Gun the engine
12 Reluctant
13 Boxer Oscar — Hoya
14 Besides
15 Hi-fi equipment
16 Tokyo mat
17 Type of energy
18 Partner of the House
24 Myra Breckenridge author
25 Answer
31 Piano man John
33 Mets' home
34 German article
35 Greek letter
36 Of a time
37 Famed German baritone
38 Mountain in Thessaly
40 Leaf pores
41 Escape hatch, with "out"
42 Capote's nickname

43 Actual being
44 Tactic
49 Ship rope
50 Upset
51 Patrick McGoohan series
52 Hart's partner
53 Switch attachment?
54 *What's My — ?*
55 Gams
57 Acted like Rich Little
58 Displays
59 PC key
61 Started
62 Capone's nemesis
63 "Uh . . . pardon me"
64 North or South
65 In debt
66 Explorer Vasco da —
67 Assam silkworm
72 French version of 18 Down
74 — majeste
77 Sioux homes
78 Alerts
79 Home of the Cuyahoga River
80 Film critic Rex
81 Scrub up
82 Followed HST
84 Yore
85 Limbaugh
86 — *the President's Men*
88 Vegas action
90 Siberian forest
91 — the fat (rehashed)
92 Braggadocio: 2 wds
93 Garb
94 Staggered
95 Ennui
96 "E" of E=mc2
97 Nuts
101 Come in
103 Stretched to the limit
104 *Born Free* lioness
106 Fortuneteller's beginning
107 Qom home
108 Somerset Maugham story
109 As regards
110 Follows mob or gang
113 Beret
114 Guido's high note
115 Modern weapon

Puzzle 2-7: Pet Shop

Across

1 Coeur d' —, Idaho
6 "Just the facts, —"
10 Bring in the crops
14 Menacing look
19 Stupefy
20 Actress Chase
21 Give off
22 Vietnam's capital
23 Stealthy thief
25 Cowboys and Indians movie, e.g.
27 Radar-gun victims
28 Monogram ltrs.
30 Not so confined
31 Singer Horne
32 "Z," in comics
33 Judy Garland's daughter Lorna
34 Netanyahu, familiarly
37 Hold in bondage
39 Soup serving, perhaps
43 Imitative, in a silly way

45 Royal topper
46 Cagney's TV police partner
47 Suffix with suburban or Manhattan
48 Participate in a swap meet
50 Losing roll in craps
52 *The Thin Man* dog
53 "— how!"
54 Wet
56 Nights before
57 Autumn color
58 Processes lumber
60 Foxy
61 Less decorated
63 In good spirits
64 Month for showers
66 Rock bottom
67 Toyota model
68 Currently a member
70 U.S. Grant cosignatory
71 Second-stringer
72 Some sofas, after conversion

75 Is in need of
76 Coiling snakes
77 Fudd of cartoondom
79 Mauna —
80 1975 Wimbledon winner Arthur
81 Simple swimming stroke
84 University board member
86 Numbered hwy.
87 The solar system's largest asteroid
88 Was in power
90 Islamic sect
91 Globe-flattening map projection
93 Subject to constraints
95 "That explains it!"
96 Pizzeria appliance
97 Army vehicles
98 Bit of wampum
100 Portrait holders
103 Fermented-honey beverages
104 Seedless raisins
108 TV-top antenna
110 Sweater with a tubular collar
112 Arctic or Indian
113 Little feller
114 Suffix with disk or cigar
115 Not — in the world
116 Is introduced to
117 Simon does it
118 Crack the books
119 Free-for-all

Down

1 First-grader's rudiments
2 "Able to — tall buildings . . ."
3 Villa d' — (Italian landmark)
4 Sadat or Begin, in 1978
5 Piano exercise
6 Itinerant, like some orchard workers
7 — *Well That Ends Well*
8 Abbr. before an alias
9 Served with tomato sauce
10 Put back to work
11 Overplay onstage
12 Puts on the radio
13 Qt. halves
14 Pie made with molasses and brown sugar
15 *In Cold Blood* writer Truman
16 Change for a five
17 Had on
18 Fact-fudger
24 Philosopher Descartes
26 Slips past
29 Kim of *Picnic*
32 Distort, as a story
33 Shoestrings
34 Rum cakes
35 Old toothpaste brand

36 Binoculars-toting hobbyist
38 Wimp
39 Cake feature
40 Circular image-producing camera accessory
41 Put into words
42 The '60s' "Turn on, tune in, drop out" adviser
44 Skirt's bottom
46 Crowbar, e.g.
49 O'Donnell of daytime TV
51 Spine-tingling
52 Lip-puckering
55 Under the weather
57 Resistance unit
59 Novelty musician Jones
61 Model airplane wood
62 Fruit drink
63 Scottish games missile
65 Homes on wheels, for short
66 Kinds of tides
67 Magna — laude
68 Waker-upper
69 Social stratum, in India
70 Slugger Maris
71 Icy forecast
73 "Death Be Not Proud" poet John
74 "Sarabandes" composer Erik
76 B, in chemistry
77 Immigrants' island
78 Scale notes
81 Hate with a passion
82 Toweled off
83 Restaurant trash receptacle
85 School counselor offering
87 Mine mishaps
89 Came out, as into society
92 Fight against
93 Tenants' contracts
94 Farmer's place, in a song
97 Sun-dried beef
99 Mr. T's TV group
100 Gift tag word
101 Kentucky Derby, for one
102 What Ali stung like
103 Poet Angelou
104 Madrid miss: abbr.
105 *Hud* Oscar-winner Patricia
106 Realtor's unit
107 — -Ball (arcade game)
109 UFO pilots
111 Colorado Indian

Puzzle 2-8: Connubial Comment

Sometimes the theme entries spell out a familiar saying or quote — such as 20, 33, 50, 69, and 84 Across.

Across

1 Hint
4 Tune
7 Electrical unit
13 Michael Jackson album
16 *The Barefoot —*
18 Arrowsmith's wife, and others
19 Rubber tree
20 Start of a quip
22 Sock end
23 Torn
24 Word with pedal
25 Noted stage couple
26 Detail
27 Actor Seagal
29 Faction
30 Poi base
32 Ruined city on the Nile
33 More of the quip
38 — o'clock scholar
39 Herr's mate
40 Will- — -wisp
41 Shade
42 Sparks or Beatty
43 Delineate
44 Unspeakable
46 Smelting matter
47 South Seas isle
48 Ankles
49 Bates of screen
50 More of the quip
54 Glee follower
56 Actress Garr's namesakes
57 Armbone
58 Brain-wave reading, for short
59 Work on wrinkles
61 Swiss artist
62 Garfield, e.g.
65 Pester

66 *Jaws* vessel
67 Unheeding
68 Amble
69 More of the quip
73 Buccaneers' home
74 Warren Beatty film
75 Indigo
76 Prim's partner
77 *Magic Mountain* author
79 Lucifer
81 Honor ender
82 B+O worker
83 One — time (singly)
84 End of the quip
88 "It had to be —"
89 Brunch order
90 Aversion
91 Likely
92 Forest tremblers
93 Feedbag tidbit
94 Language suffix

Down

1 Ponder
2 Still wrapped, as a gift
3 Ike's command
4 Egyptian dam
5 Wife of Osiris
6 WWII air arm
7 Refer to
8 Less lavish
9 Mope
10 Work units
11 Olé's kin
12 Double curve
13 Accost
14 Medicinal herb
15 Consider
16 Windlass
17 Borders
21 Root
26 George's brother
28 French wine

29 Ollie's friend
30 Gold Coast language
31 In the sack
33 Conflict ender
34 Mr. Ed, for one
35 Saclike (in botany)
36 — mater (membrane)
37 "Children should be — . . ."
39 Rank's partner
43 "Mighty — a Rose"
44 — in hand (abjectly)
45 Eyes, poetically
47 Hope
48 Corrida beast
49 Simile center
50 Destructive force
51 Huguenot center, circa 1579
52 Hebrew A
53 French article
54 Penny
55 Jacob's first
59 Path
60 Flubs
61 Ship's spine
62 Shorten
63 Taste
64 Garden bloom
67 — Tsz, Taoism founder
68 — Tsu
70 Urge
71 Triangular-sailed rig
72 Portrays
73 Lovers' meeting
76 "And I am — unto it"
77 Poet Angelou
78 Over
79 One or two follower
80 Competent
81 Minor place?
84 Evening wear
85 Hesitant sounds
86 Japanese herb
87 Possess, to a Scot

Puzzle 2-9: Phun Phor All

Across

1 Teutonic reactions
5 Tucked in
9 Type of type
14 Appear
18 Billy Crystal comedy series
19 Standard operating procedure
20 First name in copying
21 Evangelism starter
22 Change of opinion?
24 Health spas?
26 Like a factory floor
27 Horse of a certain color
28 Eagle nests
29 Ooze
30 One of the Fab Four
32 Machismo measure
33 Oscar, for one
36 Led Zeppelin
37 Your Honor, e.g.
38 Hanna-Barbera favorite?

41 Wrestler's milieu
44 Lorre role in *The Maltese Falcon*
45 Roadside sign
46 Dominate
47 Wire mesh
49 Helps out
50 The "Say Hey" Kid
51 Utah National Park
53 "My Cherie Amour" singer
54 In —
55 — *and Lovers*
56 Unidentified flying objects
57 *Laugh-In* award?
63 Closer to the beginning
64 Porthos' weapon
65 Bauxite and hematite
66 Creates bullets, in a way
67 Choir member
68 Contented sound
69 NaCl
73 Takes care of

74 *To —, With Love*
75 Chanteuse Patti
76 Shopping binge
77 Pindar specialty
78 Boys Town figure?
82 Charles' realm
84 "— Irish Rose"
85 Francis and Kevin
86 Melons
89 Less diluted
90 Vatican resident
91 Scarlett's beloved
92 Tuscan river
93 Check-out, in a way
96 Fail miserably?
98 Take-out order?
101 City on the Truckee River
102 Ham it up
103 Sounds like Porky
104 Division word
105 Once more
106 Renowned
107 Nervous
108 Ant, e.g.

Down

1 Nile nipper
2 Lawyer Roy
3 St. Peter's top
4 Austen ladies
5 "A community is like —" (Ibsen)
6 In need of a toupee
7 Freudian subject
8 LAX info
9 Sends abroad
10 "The Merry Widow" composer
11 Site of the Peacock Throne
12 Wee lad
13 One-sided, legally
14 Go on a crash diet
15 Creepy
16 *— Gantry*
17 Like many a teenager's room
19 Maintenance
23 False start
25 "Physician, — thyself"
27 Rave companion
30 Skirt features
31 Treats a hide
32 Bob's road partner
33 Dog watchdog grp.
34 Asian
35 Saharan
36 Emphasize
37 Roger Rabbit, for one
39 Rod

40 *— Magnificent Men in Their Flying Machines*
41 Enchantress of mythology
42 Turn away
43 Short and sweet
47 Won ton and minestrone
48 2.54 centimeters
50 Jazz trumpeter Davis
51 Demilitarized regions
52 *Bus Stop* playwright
53 Cracker
54 *Saturday Night Live* bits
55 Enjoys a cool one by the pool
56 Brownish orange
57 Spicy sauce
58 Hemmed and —
59 Granny on *The Beverly Hillbillies*
60 Decked out
61 *The — Is a Lonely Hunter*
62 Fairway dangers
67 Slant
68 *The — Chase*
69 E.T.'s transport
70 Jason's craft
71 — and mean
72 Perfect scores, in gymnastics
74 Beatles' hit "— a Woman"
75 Kneeler
76 Grab, at a sale
78 Place for junior
79 Like some houses on the midway
80 Historic river in Spain
81 Terminates at Cape Canaveral
82 "No time to — in the mire . . ." (Doors' lyric)
83 First victim
86 *It's a Wonderful Life* director
87 White as a ghost
88 Brandon de Wilde's plaintive cry
89 Chatter on
90 Like Dennis the Menace
92 "Thanks — !"
93 Gut feeling
94 Cream of the crop
95 Subdivision divisions
97 MD's employer
98 Author of "The Cask of Amontillado"
99 Tucked away
100 Morse code unit

Puzzle 2-10: Diamond Jubilee

Across

1 Butter servings
5 Figure atop a wedding cake
10 Super reviews
15 "I didn't —!" (suspect's line)
19 Sonny and Cher's "— You Babe"
20 "Bear" that's not really a bear
21 Leading lady Massey
22 West Point inits.
23 Baker's mix
25 Locomotive grille
27 Gladiator's workplace
28 Prayers
30 Reposition, as tires
31 Bull sounds
34 Suffix with kitchen or luncheon
35 Partner to hook and sinker
36 Simon and Garfunkel's "El Condor —"
37 "Leave it in," editorially
38 Successfully-completed negotiation
42 — Alto, California
45 Factory honcho
48 Not yet known, in a TV schedule
49 Toast topping
50 Pago Pago's land
51 Leprechaun's land
52 Like a rail, so to speak
53 Silvery fish
55 Tend to the lawn
56 Mantle's number
58 Elm offering
59 Musical acuity
60 Colossal, moviewise
62 Destiny
63 Biscuits with tea
64 One-on-one workout partner

68 Regain consciousness
71 Length x width, for a rectangle
72 Springsteen's "— Fire"
73 — *Boot* (1981 film)
76 Gorillalike
77 — Penh, Cambodia
79 Popular oil additive
80 Contaminate
82 Janet of the Clinton Cabinet
83 "— there, done that"
84 "— bleu!" (Frenchman's epithet)
86 It's forbidden
87 Prospector's find
88 Revolutionary War heroine
91 Fairway hazard
92 Raided for plunder
94 Dinesen who wrote *Out of Africa*
95 Trigonometric ratio
97 Eye woe
98 Read the bar code
99 Iridescent beetle
102 Victors of 1945
105 Without end, seemingly
108 Stereotypical pooch name
110 Wile E. Coyote's quarry
112 Vehicle in many John Wayne flicks
115 Junction point
116 "— you loud and clear"
117 Pronounce
118 Ex-champ Tyson
119 Rightmost addition column
120 Late, on a report card
121 Rhymesters
122 Roy Rogers, née Leonard —

Down

1 Type size
2 Petri-dish substances
3 Sign of affection
4 Obsolete office group
5 Transcript fig.
6 Pied Piper victim
7 Wise to the tricks of
8 Baltic Sea feeder
9 Defense contractor Martin —
10 Lasagna cheese
11 Like a hermit
12 Altar exchange
13 Abbr. at the bottom of a letter
14 Architect Eero
15 Conveyed through a pipe
16 Workplace watchdog org.
17 "— a man with seven wives . . ."
18 Truck weight, sans cargo
24 Theda of silent film fame
26 Copier additive
29 Cherry throwaway

32 Recipe amts.
33 Spicy sausages
35 Check one's mail, these days
37 Ski-resort manufacture
38 Have the nerve
39 Wharton's Frome
40 Put up with
41 Bowling center units
42 Sit for a portrait
43 — mater
44 Look like a dirty old man
46 Texaco rival
47 "When pigs fly!"
52 God with a hammer
54 Canines and incisors
56 Site of a 1692 witch-hunt
57 Kett of old comics
58 Hint for a bloodhound
61 Con's counterpart
62 Vegas card game
63 — cone (cool treat)
64 Monterrey moola
65 Au pair
66 H, spelled out
67 Force to serve, as in the military
68 Billiards bounce
69 *Carmen* or *Aida*
70 Underground worker
73 Christian of fashion
74 *The King and I* role
75 "Cool it!"
77 Martinique erupter of 1902
78 Committed a football infraction
79 Loot and pillage
81 Theater lobbies
83 Tight-fitting garment
84 Breaks a date with
85 "Layla" singer Clapton
88 More silent
89 Region of northern France
90 "No man — island . . ."
93 Comments to the audience
96 Pusher's pursuer
98 Golf's "Slammin' Sammy"
100 Benefit
101 — Thatcher (Tom Sawyer's girlfriend)
102 River through Pisa
103 Symbol of craziness
104 Fill with cargo
105 Lollapalooza
106 "Beetle Bailey" pup
107 Thurmond or Archibald of the NBA
109 Korean statesman Syngman —
111 Brady Bill-opposing org.
113 "— my drift?"
114 Hosp. trauma areas

Puzzle 2-11: Whereabouts

The entry for 9 Down is IOIOOI.

Across

1 Mans a dingy
5 — Hari
9 Philanthropist Hogg
12 Throng
17 "The Red"
18 Folksinger Phil
19 Wine: prefix
20 Actor Richard
21 Like a shish kebab's end piece?
25 Ms. Prynne
26 Quaff at the pub
27 The Ram
28 Author Alcott
30 — d'Azur
31 Woo pitcher
33 Woody's boy
35 Meet by chance
37 Trampolinists, perhaps
40 Show in Houston
41 Rorschach unit
44 Scoffer's cries
45 Unearthly
47 Swamp; bog
50 Fisheye —
51 Ancient marketplace
53 Inspires with reverence
54 Prop. deed
55 Lennon's lady
56 Beer-lover's position?
59 Manhattan and London areas
60 Party tidbits
62 Contend
63 Tension
64 Tennis great Chrissie
65 Position
67 *Turn of the —*
68 Sinks
70 Harbors
71 Sartorial types
74 Turkish titles
75 Place to saddle a camel?
80 Knock
81 Subdue, with "in"
82 Sponsorship
83 Makes uniform, with "out"
84 556, to Ovid
85 Pub container
86 Bridge feats
87 Greek war god
88 First place

89 Abhorred
91 Tree surgeon's location?
96 Attains
99 Carmelites
100 Mad as hops
102 Word with prize
103 Fill with love
105 De la Renta
107 Moines preceder
110 New York suburb
112 Result of sleeping with a torn pillow?
115 Some Japanese emigrés
116 Be a copycat
117 Arch type
118 43,560 square feet
119 Violinist Isaac
120 TV's Koppel
121 Bone: prefix
122 Oboist's need

Down

1 Ms. McEntire
2 Hershiser
3 It goes with older
4 Winter sport
5 Word with picture
6 Twinge
7 *Two Against —* (Asher travel book)
8 Drench
9 CMI
10 Internet list
11 Rollicking
12 Three, in Trieste
13 Emulate a St. Bernard
14 At the North Pole?
15 And — grow on
16 Editorial mark, for short
20 Polishing cloth
22 Clammy
23 "— saw Elba"
24 Clay pots
29 Reddish-brown
32 Diamond coups
34 Restoration of health, for short
36 Dutch city
38 Son of Odin
39 Nurtured
41 Political alliance
42 Musically, a Horne of plenty
43 Riding a tall palomino?
46 Babe's friend

48 Subjects for Freud
49 Famed crimefighter
51 States
52 Adventure tale, of old
54 Edible mushroom
56 Access, as a file
57 Skipper's call
58 — Tin Tin
59 Runaway
61 Of fowl
63 Con games
65 "— Cold" (Mick Jagger tune)
66 Macadam input
67 Shock
68 Worse than a bite
69 Author James
72 Type of review
73 Word with doctor
75 Region of Ethiopia
76 Oomph
77 Wading bird
78 Vespers chants
79 "For — jolly . . ."

82 Coffee break, in London
84 Liability
86 Fr. holy woman
87 Done to —
90 More diaphanous
92 Free of credit
93 Chinese evergreen
94 Dies —
95 School follower
96 — Ababa, Ethiopia
97 Seashore
98 Former Egyptian leader
101 Extract
104 Become downcast
106 Don't dele
108 Raison d'—
109 Molt
111 Dresden article
113 Perfect score
114 Gondolier's shaft

(crossword grid)

Puzzle 2-12

The entry for 23 Across is a type of triangle.

Across

1 Faucet problems
6 Adjective often following "Ye"
10 Precious stones
14 Houston ballplayer
19 Pay by mail
20 Press-on item
21 Kovacs regular Adams
22 Shorten again, as pants
23 Irregular geometric shape
26 Do some Thanksgiving slicing
27 Grid Hall of Famer Bobby
28 Shipbuilder's wood
29 One of the original Mouseketeers
30 Talked meaninglessly
33 Wharton deg.
35 Country star McEntire

37 Animation frames
38 Baseball's Felipe or Moises
39 Afrikaner
40 Livestock land
42 Revolutionary War monarch
48 Cheerleader's syllable
49 Some ball-carriers: abbr.
52 Posting at LAX or JFK
53 Less of a struggle
54 Secret message
56 — ware (Japanese porcelain)
58 TV host — Downey, Jr.
59 Ed Norton's workplace
60 Japanese camera brand
61 Performer
64 Fizzy drinks
65 Bill of — (shipping document)

66 "It's — real!"
67 Sign of the cross names, collectively
71 Start the kitty
72 Cartoon caveman Rubble
74 Hanker
75 Guts, as of a TV set
77 1961 Charlton Heston portrayal
78 Unlike vegetarian chili
79 Cater, in a base sort of way
81 Knight's horse
82 Old gas name
83 Hideous woman of Greek myth
84 Barbie's doll boyfriend
87 Thesaurus wd.
88 Bond creator Fleming
90 France-Russia-Britain alliance of 1907
93 Dreaded fly
96 Sunshine, slangily
97 Do, re, or mi, e.g.
98 Captain Hook's henchman
100 Russia's Itar- — news agency
102 Cleopatra's biter
103 Go all over, as kitchen grease
106 Meditation chant
108 In that case
110 Human trunks
111 Really steamed
112 "Tom Dooley" singers
118 Bushed
119 "You are —" (mall sign)
120 Spoiled kid
121 "Maria —" ('40s hit)
122 President after Grant
123 Raw metals
124 Prefix with space
125 Enjoys a novel

Down

1 A.M.A. members
2 Family room, familiarly
3 The Beatles' "— Loser"
4 Critter that can curl itself into a ball
5 Rip off
6 Upturned, as a box
7 Like the White Rabbit
8 N, S, E, or W
9 Inventor Whitney
10 Hereditary factor
11 The F.B.I.'s J. — Hoover
12 Dairy cow
13 Match, in poker
14 Sacramento's — Arena
15 Kind of warrant
16 Pair beater, in poker
17 Make merry
18 Signs of the future
24 *Steve Allen Show* regular Louis
25 Company that produced Pong
29 Comic Carvey

30 Make muffins
31 Touched down
32 — fide
33 — David (Jewish star)
34 Oktoberfest quaff
36 More exposed
39 Vivacity
41 The most populous nation
43 Metros and Prizms
44 Off-color
45 Bone: prefix
46 Harborbound in winter, perhaps
47 Cedar Rapids resident
50 *Jane Eyre* writer Charlotte
51 Burns superficially
55 Lucy's hubby
57 In — (off the ground)
58 Disney mouse
59 "Whoops! My mistake!"
61 Convent superior
62 Land, buildings, and such
63 2076, to the United States
64 Non-moving turbine part
65 He defeated Barry in 1964
68 Strong alkalis
69 Bakers get a rise out of it
70 Trace of color
73 Racing's Arcaro
76 Dropped in the mailbox
78 High-IQ group
79 Sea anemone, for one
80 Warlike god
83 Report card figs.
84 Granny or half hitch
85 Suffix with Rock or major
86 —do-well
89 "— boy!" (words of encouragement)
91 Teheran native
92 Grant right to
94 Small sofa
95 Rolle of *Good Times*
98 America's most common surname
99 *West Side Story* girl
101 Sociologist Hite
103 — voce (almost in a whisper)
104 Money player
105 Ed of *Lou Grant*
107 Riverfront Stadium team
109 Makes do, with "out"
110 Old Russian ruler
112 Even if, poetically
113 Shaq's org.
114 Coll. sr.'s test
115 Stephen of *The Crying Game*
116 Not Dem. or Rep.
117 Western treaty grp.

Puzzle 2-13: Twofers

Across

1 Tara, e.g.
6 Legs Diamond's diamonds
9 Wheeze
13 Pequod skipper
17 Have a crush on
18 — de plume (pseudonym)
19 "— the Rainbow"
20 Gloom
21 Twenty cents?
23 Stout's Wolfe
24 Tony's cousin
25 — about town
26 Iacocca
27 Dr. Salk and Dr. Spock?
29 Spotlight filter
31 Rostrum
33 Uses a soapbox
34 Hoodwinks
37 Crux
38 Alloy component
40 — glance (on a quick look)
41 "Waste not" and "want not"
44 Fido's foot
47 Recherché
49 Puts up
50 Ripsnorter
51 Cloy
52 Transforms
54 Pick on
55 Clandestine
57 Luau dish
58 Pier 21 and Pier 22?
62 — fare-thee-well
63 — out (pays)
66 Hill in San Francisco

67 Ceded
71 Mite
72 Tone
74 Do not stet
76 Calamitous
77 Legal matter
78 Marksman and shutterbug?
81 Covetousness, e.g.
82 Sees socially
83 Take — view of (look askance)
84 Ten-percenter
86 Of high peaks
89 Popcorn topping
90 A dog's — (long time)
91 Pie chart and scatter diagram?
94 Copied Osawa
96 Nancy Drew's beau
99 Destroy
100 Clay vessel
101 The Parthenon and the Sphinx?
104 Sarah — Jewett
105 Persian poet
106 From — Z
107 "Positive Thinking" preacher
108 Cole namesakes
109 Rapunzel's pride
110 All right
111 Wealth or health

Down

1 Put on the — (publicize)
2 First name
3 Author Ephron
4 Ade fruit
5 Buttons
6 *Natural Affection* author
7 Seinfeld, for one
8 Picas
9 Barrett and Jaffe
10 Allege
11 Inoculable fluids
12 Agents, e.g.
13 Snake-like
14 Nun's garb
15 Albee's *Tiny —*
16 Sanctify
22 Off one's feed
27 Plant stem's spongy center
28 Periods
30 Psychic power inits.
32 Nile fauna
34 Jeanne — (French saint)
35 A mountain state
36 Cat and dog?

37 Clutch
38 Tropical evergreen
39 Brooklyn follower
42 Earn an A
43 — runner (cuckoo's cousin)
44 Henna and indigo?
45 Gobbled
46 Sopping
48 — Gay (WWII plane)
51 Upbraid
53 "— Blas" (Lesage hero)
54 Catch in the act
56 Nice season
59 Paquin and namesakes
60 Campus mil. program
61 Plant's woody tissue
63 Letter opener
64 Till
65 Ship's cabin
68 Suffix with cash
69 Ms. Morgan of TV's *Happy Days*
70 Impression
73 Fury

74 Kind of ranch
75 Deprive a plant of sunlight
78 Throe
79 Linden and Holbrook
80 Droop
82 Arbus and Keaton
85 Aladdin's pal, et al.
86 Stage part
87 Actress Dern
88 Art reproduction
89 Windy City airport
90 1961 Susan Hayward film
92 Diva Gluck
93 Blueprint
95 Cupid
97 Hippocrates' H's
98 Excise
101 Remit
102 Hot Springs, AR, e.g.
103 Tennis unit

Puzzle 2-14: Auto-Solving

Across

1 Victory symbol
4 One of the Three Bears
8 Go for, as an opportunity
14 "— the word!" ("Shhh!")
18 Noodlehead
19 "A pity!"
20 Lead into temptation
21 Slanted type: abbr.
22 One end of a hammock, often
24 A clown may walk on them
25 Yemeni capital
26 Word before circle or sanctum
27 Bearings
29 Bottom-of-the-ninth heroics, perhaps
31 Angle measurement
33 Move on hands and knees
35 Salon job
36 Old English poet
38 "Unleaded," coffeewise

41 Rock-band schlepper
45 Alaska's 1959 achievement
50 *Sisters* actress Ward
52 In need of liniment
53 Corn-eater's throwaway
54 Most senior
57 Bit of gymnastics
60 Actor's part
62 More tearful
64 "— yellow ribbon . . ."
65 Make ashamed
67 Clad like an *Animal House* partier
69 Pepper with machine-gun fire
73 Noted Alp
76 Hook and ladder, e.g.
79 Former Clinton press secretary Myers
80 Comic Judy
82 Less loony
83 Explorer Vasco da —
85 Snake with a distinctive sound

88 Delhi dress
89 Repairman's inventory item, maybe
94 Flower — (hippies)
95 Bigger than med.
96 Ripped
97 Tide type
99 They're below ENTER and CAPS LOCK
102 Likkered up
105 Unemotional
108 Blood fluids
109 Spaceman Shepard
111 Occupied, as a lavatory
114 Ages on the vine
118 Cold weather personified
123 Baseball-card figs.
125 Eyelashes
126 Up to the job
127 Represent with symbols
129 Research group
131 Sentence subject
132 Inspire with love
133 Disappear — thin air
134 To — (perfectly)
135 Potato buds
136 Sovereign's stand-in
137 Christmas song
138 Electric-guitar pioneer — Paul

Down

1 Actress Lisi
2 Improve the text
3 Olympic dueler
4 It's 72 on many courses
5 Graduate, for short
6 Rush to sell, on Wall Street
7 Information-booth customer
8 Tenant
9 Otorhinolaryngology: abbr.
10 Suffix with system or problem
11 Aspirin unit
12 Make a scene
13 Research and development worker, maybe
14 Hodgepodge
15 Bonneville Salt Flats state
16 "The — Love" (Gershwin tune)
17 Blinds crosspiece
18 Tend to the sauce
23 Draw an outline of
28 Actor Beatty
30 —Magnon man
32 Not by a long shot
34 Laptops, e.g.
37 Barbershop symbol
39 Early nuclear org.
40 Like a pancake
42 Anonymous John
43 Ill temper
44 Slippery fish

45 "Beat it!"
46 "Sorry about that!"
47 Remove by erosion
48 Beethoven's "— Joy"
49 Kick out of the country
51 Hop out of bed
55 Any of the Declaration of Independence's 56
56 Chinese restaurant quaff
58 When on either side of "-á-," a private discussion
59 Sounds the alarm
61 Italian noble family
63 Prove erroneous
66 Shrubbery "fence"
68 Duplicates
70 "Jumpin' Jack flash, it's — . . ."
71 Concert ender
72 A Cabinet department
74 Use a harvester
75 Macho male
77 Mr. Kramden
78 Great Lakes tribesmen
81 Forty winks
84 Mars's Greek counterpart
86 Yalies
87 Send, as to a specialist
89 Ave. crossers
90 Flower holder
91 "— we having fun yet?"
92 Rouses again
93 Tit for —
98 Taro dish
100 Bit of magic
101 Marx's *Das* —
103 Subordinate Claus?
104 Sock mender
106 Pay-telephone instruction
107 Film director's "Stop!"
110 Nary a soul
112 Ellington's "— Doll"
113 Cultural: Prefix
115 Tickle pink
116 Dress to the —
117 "For Pete's —!"
118 Tarzan's love
119 Johnny Cash's "— Named Sue"
120 Whodunit board game
121 Dateless
122 No longer wild
124 Construction area
128 Freight weight
130 Cambodia's Lon —

Puzzle 2-15: The Barber-y Coast

An anagram is a rearrangement of letters to create a new word from another word — see 67 Down.

Across

1 American League batting champ
6 Right away, in the OR
10 Doesn't renew
16 Metropolitan production
17 Mrs. Julius Dithers
18 Hellos for haoles
19 Very little clothing
20 The Piltdown Man, for one
21 Most likable
22 Shore activity for barbers
25 Bandleader Kyser
26 Sept. follower
27 Rathskellar orders
28 Peripheral
30 Shore sight, barbers?
33 Playground?
36 Burrow
37 Pierre, across the Pyrenees

38 Gregory's *On the Beach* love
39 Curl one's lip at
41 Childish query
42 Gossip rag tidbit
43 Barbers in uniform?
47 Story collection: abbr.
48 Top dog in D.C.
49 "Where America shops"
50 Popular pen
51 Theater seater
53 "Nonsense!"
54 Two-faced?
56 Barber's favorite boat items
60 — *In Every Port* (Groucho film)
61 Area behind the altar
62 Michael J's *Back to the Future* mom
63 Tango quorum
64 Boats for barbers?
68 Chin cover
70 Track meet projectile

71 Scouting shelters
72 Color him green
73 — *en scene* (stage setting)
74 Dispute
75 In proper fashion: obs.
76 Land west of Nod
77 Reacts out of astonishment

Down

1 Bands of boppers
2 Individually
3 Met star Tebaldi
4 George Orwell's real first name
5 Hamper fill
6 Man of letters
7 Decathlon
8 98% of Jordanians
9 Head for the runway
10 Listlessness
11 Ryan's *Love Story* love
12 Covered with craters
13 Barber's favorite shorebird?
14 Cushy
15 BAL plane
23 Compassionate
24 Oslo native, e.g.
29 Confucian's belief
31 Carelessly spill
32 Line at the barbershop?
33 Folds
34 Declares
35 Thanksgiving sidedish

37 Tool for some cobblers
39 Seattle cager
40 Go surfing, barber-style?
41 Felt for
42 *Mr. Palomar* writer Calvino
43 Trucker's compartments
44 Type of battle
45 Man of much interest
46 Legendary archer
51 Terrorist's weapon
52 Work for charming people?
53 You can count on it
55 Fielder's cry
56 Stand against
57 Acts possessive
58 Didn't lag
59 Answers back
61 Stem sucker
63 Musical sound
65 "Woe —!"
66 For men only
67 Rhea's anagrammatic daughter
68 Lapidary specimen
69 Moray, for one

Puzzle 2-16: What Kids Say

Across

1 Scatter
6 Ill-mannered
11 Job to do
15 — *of Cancer*
17 Karmas
18 *Rio* — (1942 Abbott and Costello movie)
19 Hang around longer than Nero Wolfe's creator
21 Egyptian goddess
22 Cuban currency
23 Detroit, for one
24 Maid on *Maude*
25 8th–century invader of Spain
27 Have influence
29 Freddy Krueger's street
30 Auditor, often: abbr.
33 1981 World Series co–MVP Guerrero
36 Source of strength
38 Corned beef meals
40 Type of tide
42 Fassbinder film (1982)
43 Elliot and Nancy's son on *thirtysomething*

44 Brosnan role of the '80s
46 One–time Phoenician capital
49 Poses
50 Take a diagnostic photo of Nero Wolfe's creator
51 Had a mortgage
52 TV producer Ivan
53 Luxury car feature
54 Salt holders?
55 Glenn Close's role in *Fatal Attraction*
57 Multiplication symbol
58 Unskilled laborer
59 Winked thing
61 Author of *The Invisible Man*
63 College course: abbr.
64 Former *Jeopardy!* host Fleming
65 "Minor" place
67 Author Fleming and namesakes
69 It's left of calcium in the periodic table
71 More intimate
74 Relievers' stats
78 Roseanne Arnold's birthplace
79 Affair that lasts from Christmas Eve to the New Year, perhaps

81 "You bet," in Barcelona
82 Southwest New Hampshire city
83 Add pepper to
84 Narcissus admirer
85 Slip
86 Starts of football plays

Down

1 Period, in telegrams
2 Exam choice
3 Decomposes
4 English racetrack town
5 Person skilled in repartee
6 Mark, as a ballot
7 Book after Judges
8 Cheering
9 Finnish bathhouses
10 Air France plane, for short
11 The Bee Gees, e.g.
12 Trick played on a flight attendant, perhaps
13 Pix from flicks
14 Top name in Top 40 countdowns
16 Slender boats
20 Three rulers could make one
24 City near Lake Tahoe
26 Bet first
28 Bathroom cleaner brand
30 Chiffonier
31 Inner courtyard

32 Cigarette butts, matches, etc.
34 Hinder
35 Follow the orders of "The It Girl"
37 Southern California city
39 Annoyance
41 Give a tongue–lashing to
44 Indian title
45 A — to stand on
47 Kathie Lee's cohost
48 Henry Ford's son
50 Base of a graph
54 Naval officer, for short
56 Flair
58 Barton and 35 Down
59 Hot
60 More risky
62 Committed perjury
64 Maltreatment
66 Author Horatio
68 Convertible's counterpart
70 John Glenn's home
72 Mr. Bill's cry
73 Gang follower
75 Tabula —
76 On
77 D.C. VIPs
79 Get with great effort
80 Group that recorded the '70s album *Fragile*

Part III
Exploring Non-Crossword Puzzles

The 5th Wave   By Rich Tennant

"So you use a black marker to fill in the squares around your words? You're the same guy who cuts his jigsaw pieces to fit too, aren't you?"

Puzzle 3-1

Fill in the letter C whenever you see the letter J in the puzzle.

J B D I M   J A R M K F   T U J F :   O M   N O A   C L   N B U S S M I

_ _ _ _ _   _ _ _ _ _ _   _ _ _ _ :   _ _   _ _ _   _ _   _ _ _ _ _ _ _

D S   C K   O C Q L M Z T   Q U E M L   U   L Q U Z Z   S U J E U R M .

_ _   _ _   _ _ _ _ _ _ _   _ _ _ _ _   _   _ _ _ _ _   _ _ _ _ _ _ _ .

Puzzle 3-2

Fill in the letter O whenever you see the letter G in the puzzle.

G Y P   Y Z Y A S   G O   R   O N G R A Z Y K   Z E P I P U K   Z B   J Z B Z I N P

_ _ _   _ _ _ _ _   _ _   _   _ _ _ _ _ _ _ _   _ _ _ _ _ _ _   _ _   _ _ _ _ _ _ _

R I G J P   A S P   B Q U O R E P .

_ _ _ _ _   _ _ _   _ _ _ _ _ _ _ .

Puzzle 3-3

Fill in the letter P whenever you see the letter I in the puzzle.

I M P Y I N M P R Y   K N O W L Y W   A H X L G Y   J N   H N X K Y   J X O K   W P

_ _ _ _ _ _ _ _ _   _ _ _ _ _ _ _   _ _ _ _ _ _   _ _   _ _ _ _ _   _ _ _ _   _ _

G P R W J   N E L Y W N O A N   —   X   I X M X K P E !

_ _ _ _ _   _ _ _ _ _ _ _ _ _   —   _   _ _ _ _ _ _ _ !

Puzzle 3-4

Fill in the letter W whenever you see the letter A in the puzzle.

```
AMBCR  DNEW  WNKE  JOR  QBZRI  JAJK,  KNKNE  JCAJKE
_____  ____  ____  ___  _____  ____,  _____  _____

MJZR  EWOBIQE  JWWJTMRF.
____  _____  _____.
```

Puzzle 3-5

Fill in the letter T whenever you see the letter Y in the puzzle.

```
YANG  DOW  XDCLG:  OEY  EOG  LBOICG  JDO  DJEOI
____  ___  _____:  ___  ___  _____  ___  _____

JDOS  FNLUDOWL.
____  _____.
```

Puzzle 3-6

Fill in the letter P whenever you see the letter Q in the puzzle.

```
QUINKY  "NHQUN  OR  RZYPN"  ZYNDK  KNZY  OUBDP
_____  "_____  __  _____"  _____  ____  _____

NK  "JIRZ  JBIKO  OR  HNKO."
__  "____  _____  __  ____."
```

Puzzle 3-7

Fill in the letter P whenever you see the letter A in the puzzle.

A Q U U J Y   M D   V E L B L V F   E R G O   Q U Y   E R I I   F L U T J E   H J J A F

_ _ _ _ _ _ _   _ _   _ _ _ _ _ _ _   _ _ _ _   _ _ _   _ _ _ _   _ _ _ _ _ _   _ _ _ _ _

J U   E R X B J   B R   M Q U O .

_ _   _ _ _ _ _   _ _   _ _ _ _ .

Puzzle 3-8

Fill in the letter T whenever you see the letter Y in the puzzle.

" Y S F   J V U O   R G C C F X F V E F   Q F Y N F F V   E D W X G E F   D V R   D

" _ _ _   _ _ _ _   _ _ _ _ _ _ _ _ _ _   _ _ _ _ _ _ _   _ _ _ _ _ _ _   _ _ _   _

U G C F U J V P   W D L L G J V   G L   Y S D Y   Y S F   C J X I F X

_ _ _ _ _ _ _ _   _ _ _ _ _ _ _   _ _   _ _ _ _   _ _ _   _ _ _ _ _ _

U D L Y L   U J V P F X . "   —   J L E D X   N G U R F

_ _ _ _ _   _ _ _ _ _ _ . "   —   _ _ _ _ _   _ _ _ _ _

Puzzle 3-9

Fill in the letter T whenever you see the letter L in the puzzle.

" L O G   W G K T   N W B X T G J   Y E   Q O K L   L B   P B   Q Y L O

" _ _ _   _ _ _ _   _ _ _ _ _ _ _   _ _   _ _ _ _   _ _   _ _   _ _ _ _

N W B X T G J - E B T H G W E   K D L G W   L O G   N W B X T G J E   K W G

_ _ _ _ _ _ _ - _ _ _ _ _ _ _   _ _ _ _ _   _ _ _   _ _ _ _ _ _ _ _   _ _ _

E B T H G P . "   —   A K F   L K T G E G

_ _ _ _ _ _ _ . "   —   _ _ _   _ _ _ _ _ _

Puzzle 3-10

Fill in the letter I whenever you see the letter G in the puzzle.

```
"G  OT  SAFE  OA  OXLKOPL  TOA  NCW,  NE  PLSKPL,  G
"_  __  ____  __  _____  ___  ___,  __  _____,  _

HSKD  OW  GW  ROKJLK  WROA  OAESAL  LFVL."
____  __  __  _____  ____  _____  ____."

—  WRLSJSKL  KSSVLXLFW
—  _____  _____
```

Puzzle 3-11

Fill in the letter T whenever you see the letter Y in the puzzle.

```
"YKI  MIVOIY  FT  OBGGHGP  D  PFFA  SBMHGIMM  HM  YF
"___  _____  __  _____  _  ____  _____  __  __

LGFZ  MFEIYKHGP  GFSFAR  IWMI  LGFZM."
____  _____  _____  ____  _____."

—  DOHMYFYWI  FGDMMHM
—  _____  _____
```

Puzzle 3-12

 Fill in the letter H whenever you see the letter M in the puzzle.

```
"MUFFRPNTT   RT   MUWRPH   U   OUBHN,   OAWRPH,
"_____   __   _____   _   _____,   _____,

IOATN-QPRV   XULROS   ORWRPH   RP   UPAVMNB
_____-____   _____   _____   __   _____

IRVS."   —   HNABHN   CGBPT
____."   —   _____   _____
```

Puzzle 3-13

 Fill in the letter M whenever you see the letter O in the puzzle.

```
"OF   STRANY   HP   SKF   TABGPOSJ   LEP   LSKHM
"__   _____   __   ___   _____   ___   _____

HP   ESRY   S   DPPT   BWYMM   AM   HP   ESRY   S
__   ____   _   ____   _____   __   __   ____   _

QYL   ZATM   SKT   S   TPD."   —   NSWG   WPLSK
___   ____   ___   _   ___."   —   ____   _____
```

Puzzle 3-14

Fill in the letter I whenever you see the letter G in the puzzle.

```
"GE  BNPAP  GM  X  IGMUHBP  KPBSPPQ  X  LHMGRGXQ
"__  _____  __  _  _____  _____  _  _____
```

```
XQI  LOMPDE,  GB  GM  MPBBDPI  XLGRXKDO.
___  _____,  __  __  _____  _____.
```

```
G  SGQ!"  —  IXQQO  YXOP
_  ___!"  —  _____  ____
```

Puzzle 3-15

Fill in the letter T whenever you see the letter H in the puzzle.

```
"HOP  ACHLOPY  CD  R  BERLP  CY  TOCLO  HOPIP  RIP
"___  _____  __  _  _____  __  _____  _____  ___
```

```
RETRND  WCDLZQPICPD  HZ  GP  KRWP."
_____  _____  __  __  ____."
```

```
—  FICKZW  WP  ER  IPNYCPIP
—  _____  __  __  _____
```

Puzzle 3-16

HINT

Fill in the letter W whenever you see the letter U in the puzzle.

"URDY   RGSCY   JDXYKT   UDMD   DYWPUDW   UXZR   JMCXYT,
"____   _____   _____   ____   _____   ____   _____,

ZRDH   WXW   YPZ   QPSD   UXZR   C   KGCMCYZDD."
____   ___   ___   ____   ____   _   _____."

— JCMPY   WD   SPYZDTFGXDG
— _____   __   _____

Puzzle 3-17

HINT

Fill in the letter I whenever you see the letter W in the puzzle.

"WC   URN   JBMVE'S   PRS   BEUSJWEP   EWOV   SR   HBU
"__   ___   _____'_   ___   _____   ____   __   ___

BARNS   BEUARIU,   ORXV   HWS   EVGS   SR   XV."
_____   _____,   ____   ___   ____   __   __."

— BKWOV   FRRHVMVKS   KREPZRFSJ
— _____   _____   _____

Puzzle 3-18: 15 x 15 Squares

1 Across begins in the first square in the top row.

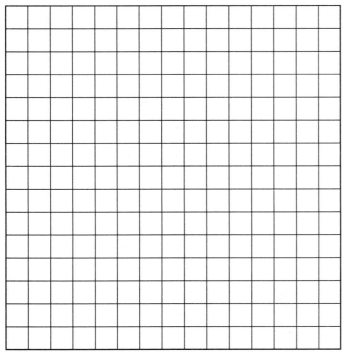

Across

1 Groom's party
5 Emirs, e.g.
10 Long-legged bird
14 Architect Saarinen
15 Aspic
16 Lose brightness
17 Companion to rare
18 Worship
19 Word with log
20 Word with President
22 " — Haw"
23 Colorado Governor
24 Barbara or Alan
26 Weimar wife
28 Syrian nomad
31 Winners: 2 wds
35 Times
36 Flower part
37 Ray of the movies
38 Neck part
39 "Simple Simon met a —"
42 Future growth for Bambi
44 Performs a sacred rite
46 Warbled
47 Wall St. inits.
48 — spumante
49 Andrew Wyeth subject

52 — Blake of *MASH:* abbr.
54 Biting
58 Neighborhood
59 More positive
61 Gum tree
62 Supermodel from Somalia
63 Catch on
64 School or collar
65 — *of the Lost*
66 Credo
67 Writing on the wall

Down

1 Like the Sahara
2 Type of duck
3 English composer
4 Winner's cry: 3 wds
5 — Kahn
6 Barnyard critter of rhyme: (2 wds)
7 — vera
8 Desolate
9 Call a poker raise
10 "—, join 'em" (born loser's lament): 5 wds
11 *Wizard of Oz* author
12 Python's Eric
13 Prophet
21 Nautical rope
23 Preoccupied
25 French article
27 First Lady Carter, to friends
28 — Flow naval base
29 — *the Family*
30 Calgary Stampede for one
32 "Scenes from —"
33 Movable home
34 Mortimer —
40 Author Seton
41 Not to scale: abbr.
42 "— *Amatoria*"
43 Talbot of "Supertrain"
45 Make fast
46 Author of *Honor Thy Father*
49 "— to the Chief"
50 Humorist Bombeck
51 Director David
53 Algerian seaport
55 Appraise
56 Steel component
57 — and dance
59 Ryker or Rutledge: abbr.
60 Acct

Puzzle 3-19: 17 x 15 Squares

1 Across begins in the fourth square in the top row.

Across

1 Wealth and good looks
7 Falls behind
11 Pertaining to a Greek philosopher
14 Sharif
15 Hemingway's mountain
18 Jay of late night TV
19 "Cherry Pie" pop singer
20 Had dinner
21 Trying to sink the Monitor
23 Lock of hair
25 Go to — (fall apart)
26 Spheres
28 Beach house
31 Dominating, as in court
34 Oldster's advantages
36 Majority vote
37 Hits and —
38 A bad case of — (jittery)
42 Business magazine
43 Actress Rigg
44 Rogers and snap
48 Teachers' org.
51 Rooney or Griffith
52 Follow the Marines
53 Brain parts in Homo sapiens
56 Influence

57 *Fried Green* —
58 American playwright James
59 Solver's aid

Down

1 "— was saying . . ."
2 Body: med.
3 Get lost, Tabby!
4 Sea eagle
5 — Mahal
6 Nova, e.g.
7 Nabokov bestseller
8 Last word
9 The Jets, e.g.
10 B'way sign
12 Retirement fund
13 Life partner
15 Economist Marx
16 Thought: pref.
17 Sappho's isle
19 Silver quality: abbr.
22 Sold, as scandals
24 Cutting ties
27 Getting along in years
28 Ringlets
29 Inter —
30 Deck post
32 Cheats
33 Cad
35 Ancient literary language
37 Socialize
39 Barn fixture
40 Split items
41 That is to — (in other words)
44 Holiday beverage in Sweden
45 Hercules' captive
46 Old time make of 54 Down
47 Better than none
48 — bene
49 Amor
50 To — (exactly)
52 Baden Baden for one
54 Auto
55 Netanyahu's land: abbr.

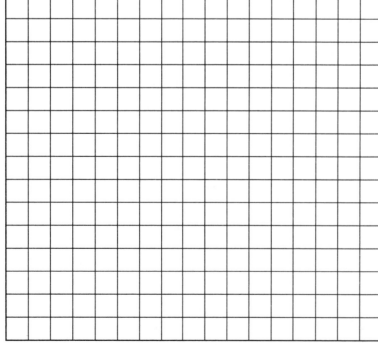

Puzzle 3-20

HINT Just to get you started, the answer to word A is PATCHOULI.

1A	2Z	█	3V	4R	5T	█	6E	7P	8Q	9K	10U	█	11N	12V	13J	█	14M	15Z	16R	17G	█
18L	19A	20K	21I	22C	█	23I	24X	25E	26K	█	27N	28A	29P	█	30H	31P	32C	33G	34Z	35K	█
36X	37T	█	38V	39R	█	40E	41F	42X	43D	44Q	45S	46B	█	47Z	48T	49W	50N	█	51H	52R	53I
54X	55B	56G	57M	58W	█	59V	60Z	61H	62P	63G	█	64F	65V	66L	█	67U	68X	69Z	70D	71A	72O
█	73Q	74X	75H	76B	77N	█	78N	79G	80J	81T	█	82N	83K	84F	85A	█	86H	87P	88A	89T	90C
91J	92S	█	93X	94S	95E	96U	97R	█	98A	99W	100M	101E	█	102T	█	103P	104M	105R	106S	107J	108Y
109L	110X	111T	█	112W	113N	114C	115F	116R	█	117G	118T	119K	120C	█	121Y	122I	123P	124M	125D	126L	█
127M	128T	129Z	█	130P	131C	132O	█	133U	134K	135B	136N	█	137X	138O	139J	140E	141R	142F	█	143V	144P
145V	█	146R	147X	148X	149L	█	150R	151Y	152M	153E	█	154A	155U	156B	157H	158S	█	159J	160H	161M	162K
163U	█	164A	165W	166N	167U	█	168Y	169M	█	170D	171P	172O	█	173L	174C	175Q	█	176W	177J	178F	█
179Z	180S	181H	182P	█	183T	184J	185O	186F	█	187Z	188L	█	189E	190Y	191K	█	192J	193D	194I	195Z	█

A Perfume oil

$\overline{88}\ \overline{71}\ \overline{164}\ \overline{98}\ \overline{85}\ \overline{1}\ \overline{19}\ \overline{154}\ \overline{28}$

B A point on a mariner's compass

$\overline{46}\ \overline{76}\ \overline{55}\ \overline{135}\ \overline{156}$

C With no outside help (2, 5)

$\overline{174}\ \overline{22}\ \overline{131}\ \overline{32}\ \overline{114}\ \overline{120}\ \overline{90}$

D Poppy product

$\overline{125}\ \overline{43}\ \overline{193}\ \overline{70}\ \overline{170}$

E Cashed in coupons

$\overline{153}\ \overline{25}\ \overline{6}\ \overline{95}\ \overline{101}\ \overline{189}\ \overline{140}\ \overline{40}$

F Bears witness

$\overline{64}\ \overline{142}\ \overline{84}\ \overline{41}\ \overline{178}\ \overline{186}\ \overline{115}$

G First movie takes

$\overline{17}\ \overline{33}\ \overline{63}\ \overline{79}\ \overline{56}\ \overline{117}$

H Unpopular presentations

$\overline{160}\ \overline{51}\ \overline{181}\ \overline{61}\ \overline{75}\ \overline{157}\ \overline{86}\ \overline{30}$

I Vibrant

$\overline{122}\ \overline{23}\ \overline{21}\ \overline{194}\ \overline{53}$

J English cutlery center

$\overline{91}\ \overline{184}\ \overline{80}\ \overline{139}\ \overline{159}\ \overline{177}\ \overline{107}\ \overline{192}\ \overline{13}$

K Teddy Roosevelt's home town (6, 3)

$\overline{83}\ \overline{191}\ \overline{26}\ \overline{9}\ \overline{35}\ \overline{162}\ \overline{20}\ \overline{134}\ \overline{119}$

L Provoked

$\overline{126}\ \overline{188}\ \overline{109}\ \overline{66}\ \overline{18}\ \overline{149}\ \overline{173}$

M Innuendo

$\overline{161}\ \overline{127}\ \overline{14}\ \overline{169}\ \overline{100}\ \overline{124}\ \overline{104}\ \overline{152}\ \overline{57}$

N Mother of King Solomon

$\overline{11}\ \overline{113}\ \overline{78}\ \overline{50}\ \overline{77}\ \overline{27}\ \overline{136}\ \overline{82}\ \overline{166}$

O Verdant

$\overline{72}\ \overline{132}\ \overline{185}\ \overline{138}\ \overline{172}$

P At wit's end

$\overline{7}\ \overline{87}\ \overline{144}\ \overline{29}\ \overline{31}\ \overline{62}\ \overline{123}\ \overline{171}\ \overline{130}\ \overline{182}\ \overline{103}$

Q On the briny

$\overline{44}\ \overline{73}\ \overline{175}\ \overline{8}$

R Fairy tale hero, with "The" (4, 6)

$\overline{105}\ \overline{97}\ \overline{16}\ \overline{146}\ \overline{150}\ \overline{52}\ \overline{4}\ \overline{39}\ \overline{141}\ \overline{116}$

S Furniture coating

$\overline{106}\ \overline{180}\ \overline{158}\ \overline{45}\ \overline{92}\ \overline{94}$

T Comedy by Aristophanes

$\overline{128}\ \overline{81}\ \overline{37}\ \overline{48}\ \overline{5}\ \overline{111}\ \overline{89}\ \overline{118}\ \overline{183}\ \overline{102}$

U Narrow strip of land

$\overline{96}\ \overline{133}\ \overline{167}\ \overline{10}\ \overline{67}\ \overline{155}\ \overline{163}$

V Smokestack

$\overline{59}\ \overline{3}\ \overline{38}\ \overline{143}\ \overline{65}\ \overline{12}\ \overline{145}$

W Palm frond

$\overline{49}\ \overline{165}\ \overline{99}\ \overline{58}\ \overline{112}\ \overline{176}$

X Snoopy

$\overline{147}\ \overline{110}\ \overline{54}\ \overline{68}\ \overline{24}\ \overline{42}\ \overline{74}\ \overline{93}\ \overline{36}\ \overline{148}\ \overline{137}$

Y Talk show hostess

$\overline{151}\ \overline{121}\ \overline{108}\ \overline{190}\ \overline{168}$

Z Of reportable interest

$\overline{2}\ \overline{195}\ \overline{179}\ \overline{34}\ \overline{47}\ \overline{15}\ \overline{60}\ \overline{69}\ \overline{187}\ \overline{129}$

Puzzle 3-21

HINT

The answer to word A is PHASEDOWN.

A Gradually reduce production (5, 4)

$\overline{121}$ $\overline{71}$ $\overline{17}$ $\overline{180}$ $\overline{130}$ $\overline{23}$ $\overline{181}$ $\overline{66}$ $\overline{184}$

B Contrasts

$\overline{172}$ $\overline{61}$ $\overline{31}$ $\overline{150}$ $\overline{53}$ $\overline{89}$ $\overline{111}$ $\overline{131}$ $\overline{155}$ $\overline{188}$

C Thin as a — (slender)

$\overline{162}$ $\overline{8}$ $\overline{6}$ $\overline{32}$ $\overline{54}$ $\overline{146}$ $\overline{44}$ $\overline{50}$ $\overline{73}$ $\overline{187}$

D Territory under the church jurisdiction

$\overline{142}$ $\overline{80}$ $\overline{70}$ $\overline{5}$ $\overline{174}$ $\overline{116}$ $\overline{144}$ $\overline{109}$ $\overline{48}$ $\overline{171}$ $\overline{185}$

E Native of Aden

$\overline{123}$ $\overline{12}$ $\overline{2}$ $\overline{46}$ $\overline{178}$ $\overline{157}$

F River to Lake Geneva

$\overline{112}$ $\overline{33}$ $\overline{164}$ $\overline{26}$ $\overline{103}$

G Acoustically reflective room (4, 7)

$\overline{163}$ $\overline{107}$ $\overline{7}$ $\overline{68}$ $\overline{28}$ $\overline{52}$ $\overline{76}$ $\overline{169}$ $\overline{11}$ $\overline{57}$ $\overline{91}$

H Mix the cards

$\overline{125}$ $\overline{45}$ $\overline{182}$ $\overline{77}$ $\overline{16}$ $\overline{159}$ $\overline{113}$

I Helpful pointer

$\overline{139}$ $\overline{42}$ $\overline{95}$ $\overline{4}$ $\overline{153}$ $\overline{136}$ $\overline{83}$ $\overline{127}$ $\overline{161}$ $\overline{37}$

J Agitated

$\overline{120}$ $\overline{100}$ $\overline{79}$ $\overline{64}$ $\overline{175}$ $\overline{129}$ $\overline{108}$ $\overline{86}$ $\overline{51}$ $\overline{96}$ $\overline{135}$

K James Garner role on TV and on film

$\overline{49}$ $\overline{21}$ $\overline{9}$ $\overline{90}$ $\overline{85}$ $\overline{147}$ $\overline{167}$ $\overline{74}$

L Award-winning costume designer (5, 4)

$\overline{166}$ $\overline{67}$ $\overline{34}$ $\overline{78}$ $\overline{98}$ $\overline{152}$ $\overline{133}$ $\overline{30}$ $\overline{143}$

M City on the Allegheny

$\overline{65}$ $\overline{158}$ $\overline{118}$ $\overline{55}$ $\overline{14}$

N Less distinct

$\overline{115}$ $\overline{106}$ $\overline{177}$ $\overline{138}$ $\overline{119}$ $\overline{60}$ $\overline{18}$

O Significance

$\overline{81}$ $\overline{141}$ $\overline{99}$ $\overline{43}$ $\overline{94}$ $\overline{151}$ $\overline{179}$

P Begrudges

$\overline{25}$ $\overline{173}$ $\overline{56}$ $\overline{137}$ $\overline{40}$ $\overline{128}$

Q US Open tennis winner, 1997 (7, 6)

$\overline{132}$ $\overline{15}$ $\overline{88}$ $\overline{22}$ $\overline{72}$ $\overline{186}$ $\overline{110}$ $\overline{176}$ $\overline{62}$ $\overline{145}$ $\overline{149}$ $\overline{170}$ $\overline{183}$

R Cuss words

$\overline{84}$ $\overline{58}$ $\overline{27}$ $\overline{134}$ $\overline{104}$ $\overline{117}$ $\overline{3}$ $\overline{97}$ $\overline{36}$ $\overline{82}$ $\overline{41}$

S Place in authority

$\overline{59}$ $\overline{87}$ $\overline{148}$ $\overline{126}$ $\overline{154}$ $\overline{168}$ $\overline{105}$ $\overline{92}$

T Little Nell in "The Old Curiosity Shop"

$\overline{38}$ $\overline{47}$ $\overline{101}$ $\overline{165}$ $\overline{140}$

U Coppola film with Matt Dillon (6, 4)

$\overline{29}$ $\overline{124}$ $\overline{19}$ $\overline{102}$ $\overline{114}$ $\overline{13}$ $\overline{69}$ $\overline{1}$ $\overline{75}$ $\overline{24}$

V Thomas Lipton, et al.

$\overline{20}$ $\overline{122}$ $\overline{63}$ $\overline{39}$ $\overline{156}$ $\overline{160}$ $\overline{93}$ $\overline{10}$ $\overline{35}$

1U		2E	3R	4I	5D	6C		7G	8C	9K	10V		11G	12E	13U	14M		15Q		16H	17A	18N	19U	20V	21K
22Q	23A		24U	25P	26F		27R	28G	29U	30L	31B	32C	33F	34L	35V		36R	37I		38T	39V	40P		41R	42I
43O		44C	45H	46E	47T	48D		49K	50C	51J	52G	53B		54C	55M	56P	57G		58R	59S	60N	61B		62Q	
63V	64J	65M	66A	67L		68G	69U		70D	71A	72Q	73C	74K	75U		76G	77H	78L	79J	80D		81O	82R		83I
84R		85K	86J	87S		88Q	89B	90K	91G	92S		93V	94O	95I	96J	97R		98L	99O	100J	101T		102U	103F	104R
105S		106N		107G	108J	109D	110Q	111B	112F	113H	114U		115N	116D	117R	118M		119N	120J		121A	122V	123E		124U
125H		126S	127I	128P		129J	130A	131B	132Q	133L	134R	135J	136I		137P	138N	139I	140T	141O	142D	143L		144D	145Q
146C	147K	148S	149Q	150B	151O		152L	153I	154S	155B		156V	157E	158M	159H		160V	161I	162C	163G	164F	165T	166L		167K
168S	169G	170Q	171D		172B	173P	174D		175J	176Q	177N	178E	179O	180A		181A	182H	183Q		184A	185D	186Q	187C	188B

Puzzle 3-22

The answer to word U is EVILTO.

A Spicy salad

$\overline{68}$ $\overline{8}$ $\overline{79}$ $\overline{144}$ $\overline{33}$ $\overline{137}$ $\overline{102}$ $\overline{55}$ $\overline{152}$ $\overline{94}$

B "Oh, I see!" (2, 2)

$\overline{129}$ $\overline{110}$ $\overline{63}$ $\overline{18}$

C Trips

$\overline{52}$ $\overline{157}$ $\overline{26}$ $\overline{92}$ $\overline{118}$ $\overline{119}$ $\overline{134}$

D Chef Julia

$\overline{54}$ $\overline{21}$ $\overline{1}$ $\overline{36}$ $\overline{71}$

E "— world!" (3, 2, 4)

$\overline{40}$ $\overline{46}$ $\overline{7}$ $\overline{91}$ $\overline{44}$ $\overline{65}$ $\overline{83}$ $\overline{145}$ $\overline{149}$

F More impoverished

$\overline{27}$ $\overline{81}$ $\overline{32}$ $\overline{75}$ $\overline{10}$ $\overline{156}$ $\overline{141}$

G Hansberry's was in the sun

$\overline{96}$ $\overline{22}$ $\overline{24}$ $\overline{117}$ $\overline{66}$ $\overline{13}$

H Choice

$\overline{150}$ $\overline{103}$ $\overline{23}$ $\overline{153}$ $\overline{99}$ $\overline{56}$

I Pre-teen

$\overline{43}$ $\overline{78}$ $\overline{100}$ $\overline{130}$ $\overline{31}$ $\overline{4}$ $\overline{89}$ $\overline{104}$ $\overline{123}$

J Rainy day hazard

$\overline{76}$ $\overline{72}$ $\overline{85}$ $\overline{87}$ $\overline{90}$ $\overline{56}$

K "Yield" to it (5, 2, 3)

$\overline{69}$ $\overline{12}$ $\overline{101}$ $\overline{139}$ $\overline{2}$ $\overline{105}$ $\overline{151}$ $\overline{82}$ $\overline{51}$ $\overline{143}$

L Guest

$\overline{60}$ $\overline{88}$ $\overline{9}$ $\overline{3}$ $\overline{124}$ $\overline{148}$ $\overline{108}$

M No coals needed here

$\overline{5}$ $\overline{93}$ $\overline{112}$ $\overline{25}$ $\overline{64}$ $\overline{126}$ $\overline{48}$ $\overline{154}$ $\overline{122}$

N TV veggie? (5, 6)

$\overline{147}$ $\overline{6}$ $\overline{29}$ $\overline{73}$ $\overline{121}$ $\overline{106}$ $\overline{111}$ $\overline{67}$ $\overline{14}$ $\overline{142}$ $\overline{125}$

O Relish

$\overline{58}$ $\overline{98}$ $\overline{28}$ $\overline{136}$ $\overline{16}$

P Nom de plume of Blair

$\overline{70}$ $\overline{128}$ $\overline{109}$ $\overline{97}$ $\overline{80}$ $\overline{47}$

Q Having errors in reasoning

$\overline{135}$ $\overline{45}$ $\overline{114}$ $\overline{42}$ $\overline{38}$ $\overline{19}$

R Summer destroyers

$\overline{138}$ $\overline{17}$ $\overline{35}$ $\overline{57}$ $\overline{127}$ $\overline{77}$ $\overline{133}$ $\overline{61}$

S Volunteer's statement (3, 2, 2)

$\overline{140}$ $\overline{120}$ $\overline{11}$ $\overline{116}$ $\overline{84}$ $\overline{53}$ $\overline{49}$

T Valley

$\overline{30}$ $\overline{37}$ $\overline{41}$ $\overline{131}$ $\overline{115}$ $\overline{74}$

U Foodini's first two words to Pinhead (in English) (4, 2)

$\overline{59}$ $\overline{155}$ $\overline{86}$ $\overline{107}$ $\overline{62}$ $\overline{113}$

V Salome's last veil

$\overline{39}$ $\overline{146}$ $\overline{34}$ $\overline{132}$ $\overline{15}$ $\overline{20}$ $\overline{50}$

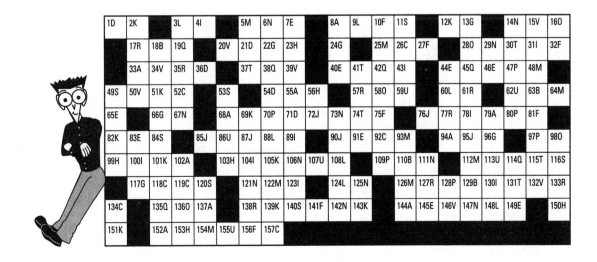

Part IV
The Part of Tens

The 5th Wave   By Rich Tennant

"You've been so grumpy since you haven't been able to figure out that stupid six-letter word for malcontent!"

In this part . . .

People cannot exist on puzzles alone! Especially when there is so much more to enjoying puzzles than actually working them. In this part, I take you beyond the puzzle grid into the wider world of puzzledom. Specifically, I discuss some reference books to help you out when you need a little nudge (okay, I give you tips on how to cheat), and I take you on a quick tour of puzzles from different parts of the world.

Chapter 1
Ten Puzzle Tools to Help You through the Rough Spots

*T*he concept of cheating doesn't exist in puzzle solving. If you derive pleasure from browsing through reference books in search of an answer, then that search is all part of the way you play the game. Whether you answer the clues right off the bat or you turn to another source (meaning a dictionary or simply someone else within earshot) depends on your personal taste. Besides, even if you do cheat, who knows except you?

Professional acrossionado Stan Newman attributes his outstanding career as a puzzle tournament winner to hitting the books. The key to puzzle prowess? Looking it up! — whatever *it* is. A healthy curiosity about words and where they come from helps you build a strong vocabulary that serves you well puzzle after puzzle.

In this chapter, I tell you about the four basic reference guides for the confirmed and novice acrossionado. These references should give you the boost you need when you hit the wall on a particularly sticky clue.

Word Finders to the Rescue!

A *word finder* provides combinations of letters that supply the missing letters to an entry you are trying to complete. The word finder lists partially completed entries alphabetically by number of letters per word, ranging from two to seven letters. When you open a word finder, you see incomplete word fragments joined by blanks. For each fragment, the word finder lists all the possibilities that use the letters you know.

Some crossword dictionaries include an abridged word finder in an appendix, which can be extremely helpful; you can read more about crossword dictionaries in "Flipping for Answers in a Crossword Dictionary" in this chapter.

If you feel flush due to a windfall, go for the ultimate word finder, called *The Crossword Answer Book,* by Stan Newman and Daniel Stark, published by Time Books ($27.95). This ambitious tome simply lists every possible configuration of puzzle entry that you may ever encounter. If you have an unfinished entry that looks like *H*F* (with each * representing a missing letter), the *Answer Book* is the place to find every possible answer. I recommend this book for the following reasons:

> ✔ It contains 650,000 entries (no clues) in alphabetical order by number of letters, making the book very comprehensive and easy to use. The *Answer Book* lists three- to seven-letter entries, arranged by word length and sorted by two given letters per category.

> ✔ The *Answer Book* includes not only common two-word phrases but also full names, such as ED ASNER and KEY WEST.

Matching Clues and Entries in Crossword Keys

When you have no idea what the answer to a clue may be, and you don't have even a single connecting letter to inspire you, consider heading to the shelf for a crossword key.

A *crossword key* matches common entries with common crossword clues. Typically, a crossword key offers one entry per clue, which you find organized by clues.

For example, if you come across a clue like "Brit. weapon" and the four-letter entry escapes you, you may find the answer by looking up the clue in the key, looking under B. The key should give you the entry, which is STEN.

Flipping for Answers in a Crossword Dictionary

A crossword dictionary doesn't explain what a word means or how to use it. This kind of dictionary matches parts of common clues with typical entries listed by number of letters. You look up a word in the clue that's stumping you and find a list of common entries sorted by number of letters per entry. For example, if you look up a typical clue like "Flower part," you find a series of entries beginning with four letters at STEM, and escalating through AMENT and COROLLA. You can then select the entry that best suits your grid.

Many times, the editors of the crossword publications that you find in the bookstore compile crossword dictionaries. Your best bet is to buy the companion dictionary to the crossword publication you buy, because then your clues and definitions are drawn from the same database. In other words, if you're a *Dell Puzzle Magazine* fan, you may want to invest in the *Dell Crossword Dictionary,* which hasn't gone out of print since its debut in 1950.

If you're looking for a comprehensive crossword dictionary, here's a list of recommended ones:

> ✔ *A to Z Crossword Dictionary,* by Edy Garcia Schaffer (Putnam, $21.95; Avon, $5.99): An alphabetical listing of 225,000 clue words and their possible entries

> ✔ *Andrew Swanfeldt Crossword Puzzle Dictionary,* 6th Edition (Harper Books, $15): An alphabetical listing of clues with possible entries presented by number of letters

> ✔ *The Master Crossword Puzzle Dictionary,* by Herbert Baus (Doubleday, $24.95): Highly regarded by industry insiders, this dictionary includes 200,000 clue words and one million answer words arranged alphabetically and by length.

> ✔ *New York Times Dictionary,* edited by Tom Pulliam and Clare Grundman (Times Books, $27.50; paperback, $17): Includes multiword entries and shaded boxes that highlight geographical clues and entries

> ✔ *Random House Crossword Puzzle Dictionary* (Random House, $23; Ivy Books, $5.99): An alphabetical listing of 700,000 clues and answers that features geographical locations in shaded boxes

- *USA Today Crossword Dictionary*, edited by Charles Preston and Barbara Ann Kipfer, (Hyperion, $12.95): A compilation of clues from the pages of the newspaper with emphasis on names and nouns, organized by main subjects with related subgroups

- *Webster's New World Dictionary*, edited by Jane Shaw Whitfield (Macmillan, $20; paperback, $12.95): In addition to the alphabetical listing, a special feature in the back of the book highlights topics of puzzle interest by section (Bible, chemistry, Supreme Court, and so on).

- *Webster's New World Easy Crossword Key*, edited by James H. Capps (Simon and Schuster, $10.95): Includes 155,000 puzzle clues matched with entries, as well as helpful supplements that list missing-word clues and clues that begin with numerals

If you'd rather have a crossword dictionary that you can carry around with you (some of the more comprehensive guides are rather large and heavy), consider one of the following handy pocket crossword dictionaries:

- *Crossword Busters*, by James Dykes (Berkley, $5.99): A compact reference sorted by categories from alphabets to zodiac signs

- *The New York Times Concise Crossword Dictionary*, by Tom Pulliam, Clare Grundman, and Gorton Carruth (Warner Books, $5.99): A portable, abridged version of *The New York Times Dictionary*

- *Random House Concise Crossword Puzzle Dictionary* (Warner Books, $6.99): An abridged version of the comprehensive volume

Word Finder-Dictionary Hybrids

If you're not sure which type of solving help you need, then you may benefit from a combination word finder-dictionary. Here are two good ones:

- *Dell Crossword Dictionary*, revised by Wayne Robert Williams (Dell Books, $5.99): A combination reference that includes three sections: clues and their definitions in alphabetical order, special sections on topics of crossword interest (sports teams, a name finder, and more), and a word finder for three- and four-letter words. Updated in 1994, it's pocket-sized and convenient to carry.

- *New American Puzzle Dictionary*, edited by Albert and Loy Morehead (Signet, $5.99): A "classic" reference from the man who introduced the Puns and Anagrams style puzzle. This book offers more than 150,000 words divided into three sections: clues and their definitions in alphabetical order, special sections on topics of interest, and a word locator (same thing as a word finder) for words of two to four letters. The book also includes tips on solving cryptic crossword puzzles.

When All Else Fails . . .

A puzzle editor's job is to offer you enough information on the page to help you through the grid on your own steam. On the other hand, part of the fun of solving is refreshing your memory on certain subjects.

Reference books beyond dictionaries or word finders round out a puzzler's library. I find the following "other" references to be especially helpful:

- *Benet's Reader's Encyclopedia,* by William Rose Benet and Bruce Murphy (HarperCollins, $35): Many people consider this book to be the most comprehensive guide to world literature on the market.

- *The Billboard Book of Top 40 Hits,* by Joel Whitburn (Billboard Directories, $19.95): In addition to the great photographs provided throughout the book, you can find all kinds of popular music trivia in this reference.

- *Information Please Almanac* (Houghton Mifflin, $10.95): An almanac is a handy guide when you're grasping at straws on topics relating to celebrities, current events, or even geography. The 1997 edition features a special crossword puzzle section called "First Aid to Crossword Puzzlers." Highlights include common crosswordese as well as key names from the Bible and ancient mythology. (I prefer an up-to-date edition of *Information Please* as a reference to current celebrities because I'm forever forgetting whether Liv Ullmann spells her surname with one or two N's.)

- *Leonard Maltin's Movie and Video Guide* (Signet, $7.99): No matter how often you see a film or hear a name, you need to check spelling from time to time. Maltin includes a movie-title index for stars and directors. Besides, you need a source to help with those clues that refer to the Oscars.

- *Total Television: The Comprehensive Guide to Programming from 1948 to the Present,* by Alex McNeil (Penguin USA, $29.95): If you think that descriptions of 5,400 series and their major participants from the years of 1948 to 1995 may help you in your solving, then pick up this book. Besides, it makes interesting light reading.

- *The World Almanac* (St. Martin's Press, $9.95): The standard almanac everyone's used since school days. It works! If you really want to know where to find a crossword peak or valley, an atlas may help. But you can usually find geographical answers in your other references.

Finding It All on the World Wide Web

Those of you who are lucky enough to be connected to the World Wide Web already have access to just about any reference material a puzzler could need — for free! Even if you aren't a Web head, you may have already heard about the wealth of information available out there in Cyberspace; you can find out what you need to know about the most obscure topics you can imagine, including aliens, recipes for fish stew, and video games.

Most important to the puzzler is that you can search the World Wide Web and Web sites to find very specific information. For example, if you come across a clue that's really stumping you, you can fire up your browser, plug in the key words from the clue, and surf until you find an answer. (If you need a little help on your Web searching skills, pick up a copy of *World Wide Web Searching For Dummies,* by Brad Hill, published by IDG Books Worldwide, Inc.)

Chapter 2

Ten Puzzles from around the World

*O*ver time, crosswords have crossed many borders to other lands. Although the basics of crosswords — grids and clues — translate well, the way they combine differs as you leave the American style, as you may have already observed with the British cryptic crossword.

Puzzles in other languages give you a chance to put to use what you may have picked up through the lexicon of foreign crosswordese. Even if you never venture into this territory, foreign puzzles may give you some new insights into the American-style crossword.

When you think of crosswords, the image is a black-and-white diagram within a square grid. The checkered pattern is symmetrical. (If you hold the puzzle upside-down, the pattern remains the same.) Some white squares have numbers that correspond to clue numbers, which are sorted in Across and Down columns. Every letter *interlocks,* which means that each letter participates in two words, one Across and another Down.

In puzzles of different languages, you find a different set of standards. Some main differences include:

✔ **Asymmetrical patterns:** Mirror images are not required in some grids.

✔ **Clues:** Sometimes clues are listed within the grid without numbers.

✔ **Unchecked letters:** Complete interlock is not the rule.

✔ **No themes or puzzle titles:** Entries do not relate to each other.

✔ **Dictionary definitions:** These are the rule rather than the exception.

✔ **Square cutouts:** Some languages insert cartoons into the center of the grid.

Different languages obviously allow for different types of letter combinations. The letter E, which is so popularly used in English language crosswords, fades into the background in other languages.

Curiously, crosswords in other languages don't borrow from English for their entries. (English-language puzzles often borrow a word or two from other languages.)

Many countries have versions of the crossword. From *crucigramas* (Spain) to *les mots croises* (France), acrossionados have their bases covered. In this chapter, I give you a brief tour of these great puzzles.

Arabic Crosswords

Puzzles in Arabic feature the following characteristics:

- ✔ **The grid:** Numbered from right to left, the grid is usually 9 x 9 squares. The language reads from right to left, and the same principle applies to crosswords. You find the first Across clue in the upper-right corner of the grid.
- ✔ **The clues:** Dictionary definitions rule the clues.

In addition to crosswords, Arabic solvers enjoy fill-ins. Even if you don't read the language, you may be able to set the correct letters into the squares as you would piece together a jigsaw puzzle.

Vowels are not treated as letters but as notations connected to consonants. As a result, the grid is filled with consonants only.

Crucigramas: Solving Spanish Style

When in Spain, you can look forward to the following solving challenges:

- ✔ **The grid:** Features asymmetrical patterns and some bar diagrams.
- ✔ **The clues:** Most clues are dictionary definitions.

A popular Spanish variation on the conventional American crossword lists clues in a different system. In this variation, the crossword ends up looking like a graph. Rather than number each clue in the square, *crucigramas* organize the grid outside the grid's squares. Across the top row, numbers are listed one to a column; down the left side, each row is assigned a Roman numeral. Each clue is referred to by the combination of two elements; for example, VII-8 to indicate seven rows down, eighth box across.

Some *crucigramas* appear familiar in layout to what you find stateside: Grids with numbers that correspond to clues listed beside the diagram. You match the number of the clue to the place in the grid where the entry belongs.

You're not looking at Across and Down clues when working Spanish crosswords. Instead, you find *Horizontales* and *Verticales*.

You can find crosswords in *Catalan*, a special dialect spoken in the eastern part of Spain.

In addition to *crucigramas*, Spanish constructors also produce acrostics and diagramlesses for their acrossionados.

Hebrew Solving

When solving in Hebrew, you encounter the following challenges:

- ✔ **The grid:** Typically, the gird measures 11 x 13 squares with unchecked letters. Because the Hebrew language reads from right to left, so do the crossword grids; the first Across clue lies in the top-right corner rather than the accustomed top-left corner.

- ✔ **The clues:** Dictionary definitions are the order of the day when it comes to most clues.

Only consonants are inserted in the grid, according to the way the Hebrew written language presents vowels as notations attached to consonants.

Japanese Solving

If you speak Japanese, you can look forward to the following features when you pick up a crossword puzzle:

- ✔ **The grid:** Typically, the grid measures 8 x 8 squares. Solving in Japanese involves symbols, rather than letters, using the *hiragana* writing system.

- ✔ **The clues:** Dictionary definitions dominate the clues.

The *hiragana* system consists of 51 symbols, each of which represents a syllable.

Kreuzwortratsel: Solving German Style

The German-style puzzle, called a *Kreuzwortratsel,* has the following features:

- ✔ **The grid:** Unlike the typical square grids that most English-language puzzle use, the *Kreuzwortratsel* appears usually as a rectangular grid.

- ✔ **The clues:** Inserted in the blank squares of the grid, with arrows indicating the entry direction. Clues are sorted by numbers across the top row instead of inserting numbers into the white squares. You're not looking at Across and Down in a German crossword: The terms are *Waagrecht* and *Senkrecht*.

German crosswords include at least one unchecked letter per entry. The lack of overall interlock enhances the challenge.

German puzzles accommodate vowels that include an umlaut accent (two dots above the vowel) by adding an E after the vowel.

The typical German puzzle is all in one: The grid contains clues right in the squares. Instead of black squares, clues are listed in these empty boxes with arrows pointing in the direction of the entry. Gone are the black-and-white patterns. Instead, you find that each blank square in the German crossword contains a clue or two. Sometimes the clue squares are shaded to differentiate them from the entry squares. Due to the tiny size of the square, the clue is usually just one word. German puzzles are narrow and long, without symmetrical patterns.

You may try the German-style puzzle in English. *Games* magazine has adapted this style of puzzle as a regular feature dubbed "Pencil Pointers."

Kryss: Solving Scandinavian Style

The Scandinavian *kryss* has many of the same traits as the German *Kreuzwortratsel* (see "Kreuzwortratsel: Solving German Style" in this chapter for the details).

What's special about this puzzle is the presentation. At the center of the grid you find a graphic (a photograph or cartoon), which serves as a clue for one or more entries. The entry may end up to be a caption for the picture. (American solvers may see a comparison between the *kryss* and the jumble — both involve a cartoon with a series of related words in a scrambled form.)

For the fluent Swedish solver, there is a cryptic crossword format.

Mot Croises: Solving French Style

French-language puzzles typically sport the following features:

✔ **The grid:** Typically, the grid is an asymmetrical pattern in a small, rectangular grid (usually 9 x 11 squares). Rather than Across and Down designations, the grid is divided by columns. Across the top, the columns are numbered from 1 through 11. Down the side, each row is assigned a Roman numeral. By finding the intersections, you solve the clues.

✔ **The clues:** Dictionary definitions characterize most clues. In a French crossword, instead of Across and Down you have clues that read *Horizontalement* and *Verticalement*.

Modern art seems to have influenced the way the French construct their puzzles. Perhaps because the *mot croises* contains many two-letter entries, the overall impression is more staccato than in American puzzles. (Two-letter entries may not be words but letter combinations or abbreviations.)

Symmetry and complete interlock are not required in the grid. Each entry contains at least one unchecked letter.

Parole Incrociate: Solving Italian Style

When passing the time in the piazza with an Italian crossword puzzle, you can look forward to the following features:

✔ **The grid:** You find asymmetric patterns in a rectangle or bar grids with unchecked letters.

✔ **The clues:** Italian crossword clues are designated like the American type as Across (*orizzontali*) and Down (*verticali*). Because the language includes many long words (over six letters), crosswords reflect this by featuring "fields of white."

L'Enigmistica, which comes out weekly, is the most popular Italian puzzle magazine in the country. Every page features a crossword or riddle, including the cover.

You won't find the letter E in final position as often in Italian as in the English language.

Stavrolexo: Solving Greek Style

The Greek-style puzzle offers the following features:

✔ **The grid:** Mostly, you see rectangular grids with unchecked letters.

✔ **The clues:** Most of the clues are straightforward dictionary definitions.

In Greece, you have a choice between the Italian- and French-style crosswords. In fact, you may find puzzles that have clues in Greek with entries in French.

Part V
Appendixes

The 5th Wave   By Rich Tennant

"Oh them? They create and sell crossword puzzles for a living."

In this part . . .

After you finish a puzzle (or after you find it impossible to resist the temptation to cheat), turn to Appendix A in this part to find out the answers that inquiring minds want to know. In Appendix B, I tell you everything you need to know about working the puzzles you find in Part III of this book, including cryptograms, diagramlesses, and acrostics.

Appendix A

Answers

Puzzle 1-1

Page 6

H	A	H	A		P	A	W	E	R		C	A	N	T
E	T	O	N		A	S	I	D	E		O	L	E	O
R	O	U	G	H	R	I	D	E	R		A	L	G	A
S	P	R	E	E			O	N	A		L	I	E	D
	G	R	E	E	N	W	I	T	H	E	N	V	Y	
M	E	L		D	E	E		C	E	E	S			
A	L	A	S		L	A	B			S	C	E	N	E
M	I	S	C		S	T	O	C	K		E	X	E	C
A	E	S	O	P			B	A	N		S	P	O	T
			R	O	S	S		F	E	Z		U	N	O
H	O	L	E	I	N	T	H	E	W	A	L	L		
A	L	E	C		A	R	A		P	A	S	T	A	
D	I	V	A		P	I	N	C	U	S	H	I	O	N
O	V	E	R		A	D	D	O	N		T	O	O	T
N	E	R	D		T	E	S	T	S		I	N	K	S

Puzzle 1-3: Calling Earth

Page 8

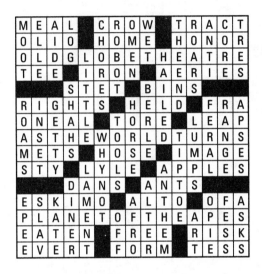

M	E	A	L		C	R	O	W		T	R	A	C	T
O	L	I	O		H	O	M	E		H	O	N	O	R
O	L	D	G	L	O	B	E	T	H	E	A	T	R	E
T	E	E		I	R	O	N		A	E	R	I	E	S
			S	T	E	T		B	I	N	S			
R	I	G	H	T	S		H	E	L	D		F	R	A
O	N	E	A	L		T	O	R	E		L	E	A	P
A	S	T	H	E	W	O	R	L	D	T	U	R	N	S
M	E	T	S		H	O	S	E		I	M	A	G	E
S	T	Y		L	Y	L	E		A	P	P	L	E	S
			D	A	N	S		A	N	T	S			
E	S	K	I	M	O		A	L	T	O		O	F	A
P	L	A	N	E	T	O	F	T	H	E	A	P	E	S
E	A	T	E	N		F	R	E	E		R	I	S	K
E	V	E	R	T		F	O	R	M		T	E	S	S

Puzzle 1-2: Words Ending in "TION"

Page 7

L	O	N	G		C	L	A	I	M		A	C	T	S
O	D	O	R		R	I	N	G	O		B	O	I	L
A	D	M	I	R	A	T	I	O	N		A	N	N	E
	S	E	N	A	T	E		T	O	A	S	T	E	D
			T	E	R		P	I	E	R				
R	A	D	N	E	R		D	O	O	R		I	V	E
I	D	E	E	S		C	U	R	L	Y		T	E	A
L	O	F	T		F	A	N	C	Y		S	I	R	S
E	R	I		R	A	N	C	H		D	O	O	N	E
D	E	N		E	R	S	E		S	I	N	N	E	D
		I	C	E	R		S	H	A					
A	U	T	O	M	A	T		H	A	N	S	E	L	
G	L	I	B		G	E	N	E	R	A	T	I	O	N
O	N	O	R		U	T	I	L	E		E	R	G	O
N	A	N	A		T	E	L	L	S		T	E	E	D

Puzzle 1-4: Playing Bridge

Page 9

E	B	B	S		N	A	D	E	R		A	D	E	E
Q	U	I	T		O	L	I	V	E		J	A	V	A
U	R	G	E		F	I	V	E	S	P	A	D	E	S
A	L	O	M	A	R		E	N	T	I	R	E	L	Y
L	S	T		L	I	S		T	E	X				
			D	E	L	T	A		D	E	B	A	T	E
F	O	U	R	C	L	U	B	S		L	E	M	O	N
A	S	T	I		S	N	O	W	S		G	I	R	D
S	L	E	E	P		T	W	O	H	E	A	R	T	S
T	O	S	S	E	S		L	O	R	A	N			
			T	E	D		N	O	R		A	B	C	
R	E	W	A	R	D	E	D		U	L	S	T	E	R
O	N	E	D	I	A	M	O	N	D		A	R	E	A
O	D	I	E		N	O	T	R	E		R	I	T	Z
M	O	R	N		S	N	E	A	D		A	P	S	E

Puzzle 1-5: Initial Offerings
Page 10

Puzzle 1-7
Page 12

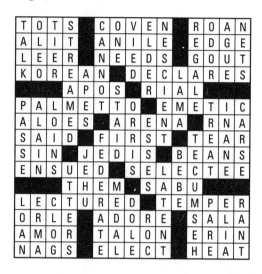

Puzzle 1-6: Hiss!
Page 11

Puzzle 1-8: Musical Hotshots
Page 13

Puzzle 1-9: Comparatively Speaking

Page 14

Puzzle 1-11: Says Who?

Page 16

Puzzle 1-10: Getting Directions

Page 15

Puzzle 1-12: Up in the Air

Page 17

Puzzle 1-13: Gumshoe
Page 18

Puzzle 1-15: Do's and Dont's
Page 20

Puzzle 1-14: Friends of Horatio Hornblower
Page 19

Puzzle 1-16: Greetings
Page 21

Puzzle 1-17: Triads

Page 22

O	K	A	Y			O	F	F			A	M	M	O
P	O	C	O		S	A	R	I		C	L	E	A	N
T	O	M	D	I	C	K	A	N	D	H	A	R	R	Y
S	P	E	E	C	H		T	A	R	E		L	E	X
			L	E	O	N		L	I	E	D			
S	O	S		S	L	O	P		P	R	O	P	E	R
E	T	N	A		A	S	I	A		I	N	A	N	E
T	H	E	T	H	R	E	E	S	T	O	O	G	E	S
T	E	R	R	E		S	T	I	R		R	E	M	O
O	R	D	E	A	L		A	D	A	M		S	Y	D
			E	D	I	E		E	C	O	N			
S	O	L		P	O	G	O		T	R	I	C	K	S
T	H	E	K	I	N	G	S	T	O	N	T	R	I	O
U	N	I	O	N		A	L	A	R		R	I	L	L
B	O	A	S			R	O	B			O	B	O	E

Puzzle 1-18: Who's Zoo in Fashion

Page 23

S	T	O	P	S			F	E	T	A			F	A	B
T	H	R	E	A	D		A	L	A	R		E	S	L	
P	O	O	D	L	E	S	K	I	R	T		A	T	A	
			T	R	E	E		P	O	S	T	E	R	
D	E	C	A	Y		L	O	G		O	C	H	R	E
B	E	L	L		L	A	U	R	A		R	E	N	D
L	L	A	D	R	O		T	A	R	T	A	R		
	S	M	E	A	R	S		F	L	A	M	B	E	
		D	R	O	N	E	S		E	M	B	O	S	S
M	A	I	M		E	L	L	I	S		L	A	S	E
E	D	G	E	R		L	E	O		B	E	S	O	T
S	I	G	N	I	N		E	N	D	O			
H	E	E		M	O	N	K	E	Y	S	U	I	T	S
E	U	R		E	L	E	E		E	S	P	I	E	S
S	S	S		S	O	A	R		A	S	I	A	N	

Puzzle 1-19: Arthur Murray Studio

Page 24

A	B	E	T		A	S	P	I	C		E	T	C	H
M	E	I	R		C	L	A	S	H		T	H	E	O
T	A	R	A	N	T	E	L	L	A		A	E	R	O
	R	E	P	A	I	D		E	R	U	P	T	E	D
			S	O	S			G	R	E	W			
N	A	T	H	A	N		W	R	E	N		O	L	D
A	V	A	I	L		P	I	E	R	S		S	E	A
O	O	P	S		S	A	R	A	S		E	T	A	L
M	I	D		C	I	T	E	D		S	T	E	V	E
I	D	A		O	D	E	S		S	L	O	P	E	S
			N	O	D	E		S	T	U				
R	A	C	I	E	S	T		T	A	R	R	E	D	
A	S	I	N		H	O	K	E	Y	P	O	K	E	Y
P	I	N	K		O	R	A	L	E		P	E	L	E
S	A	G	S		W	A	N	E	D		E	D	I	T

Puzzle 1-20: Ag-gies

Page 25

M	A	R	C	O		O	A	T	H		S	C	A	M
A	N	E	A	R		F	L	A	Y		A	R	L	O
S	T	E	R	N		F	I	R	M		L	E	I	S
S	I	L	V	E	R	S	T	O	N	E		A	B	E
			E	R	A		S	A	L	A	M	I	S	
M	O	T		Y	V	E	S		L	I	M	P		
A	S	H	E		E	N	N	S		H	O	U	S	E
T	H	E	S	I	L	V	E	R	S	U	R	F	E	R
T	A	R	T	S		Y	E	T	I		E	F	T	S
		E	E	L	S		R	A	T	A		S	S	E
S	O	I	R	E	E	S		A	T	E				
E	N	V		S	I	L	V	E	R	H	E	E	L	S
R	E	E	D		Z	I	O	N		E	R	R	O	L
V	A	R	Y		E	C	T	O		N	I	T	R	E
E	L	S	E		D	E	E	S		S	E	E	D	Y

Puzzle 1-21: Primrose Path

Page 26

```
P O W D E R E D ■ A R E O L A
A N A E R O B E ■ C A R D E D
Y E L L O W B R I C K R O A D
S A T ■ S E E ■ G R E E R ■
■ ■ G I R D ■ N E R D ■
A U D I O S ■ A I D S ■ E P I
S T E R N ■ A S T I ■ O X E N
H I L L S T R E E T B L U E S
E L L S ■ A T A D ■ A D D L E
S E A ■ U N I T ■ P R I E S T
■ ■ O R G S ■ N O N E ■
■ T I B E T ■ O P A ■ S R O
T W O L A N E B L A C K T O P
R E G E N T ■ E A R L I E S T
A D O R E S ■ E N T E N T E S
```

Puzzle 1-23: Solid Solving

Page 28

Puzzle 1-22: Doing the Wave

Page 27

Puzzle 1-24: A Day at the Beach

Page 29

Puzzle 1-25: All-Inclusive
Page 30

Puzzle 1-26: Jewelry Store
Page 31

Puzzle 1-27: Mixed Signals
Page 32

Puzzle 1-28: Partners
Page 33

Puzzle 1-29: And So to Bed
Page 34

A	S	H	E		G	L	U	M		O	P	E	R	A
S	H	A	M		R	U	S	E		P	E	P	Y	S
P	A	R	B	O	I	L	E	D		T	R	E	A	T
S	H	E	E	T	M	U	S	I	C		R	E	N	I
			D	O	A				C	O	T	Y		
D	A	N		E	L	B	A		T	O	K	Y	O	
I	R	A	Q		D	E	B	I		M	I	A	M	I
S	E	C	U	R	I	T	Y	B	L	A	N	K	E	T
C	A	R	E	Y		A	S	I	A		G	O	G	O
	S	E	E	N	A		S	S	G	T		V	A	N
		N	E	L	L			O	A	S				
H	A	R	M		P	I	L	L	O	W	T	A	L	K
U	B	O	A	T		C	O	U	N	S	E	L	O	R
C	L	A	R	E		I	S	L	A		A	L	P	O
K	E	N	Y	A		T	E	L	L		M	S	E	C

Puzzle 1-31: Spring Training
Page 36

Puzzle 1-30: What Was That Again?
Page 35

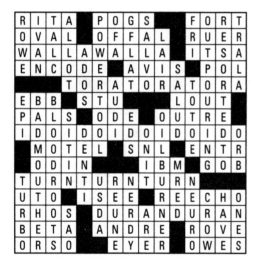

Puzzle 1-32: Conversation Pieces
Page 37

Puzzle 1-33: EN Words
Page 38

E	V	I	T	A		A	B	R	A		E	D	D	A
G	E	T	E	M		N	O	E	L		N	A	I	L
A	R	E	N	A		A	R	M	I	S	T	I	C	E
D	A	M	O	Z	E	L		O	V	E	R	S	E	E
		R	E	C	O	N	V	E	N	E				
P	A	T	S		O	G	E	E		I	N	G	L	E
E	L	A		C	L	U	E		O	C	E	A	N	
C	A	M	E	L		E	D	S		R	H	E	T	T
A	M	I	N	O			L	E	A	S		S	E	R
N	O	L	A	N		R	E	A	L		A	E	R	Y
		M	E	T	E	R	M	A	I	D				
A	M	P	E	R	E	S		L	I	N	D	E	N	S
M	I	L	L	S	T	O	N	E		D	E	V	I	L
E	R	I	E		E	L	I	S		I	R	E	N	E
N	E	E	D		S	E	T	S		A	S	S	A	Y

Puzzle 1-34
Page 39

	P	A	T	I	N	A		M	E	D	D	L	E
P	A	L	A	V	E	R		O	L	D	I	E	S
U	S	E	L	E	S	S		P	I	A	N	I	S	T
S	T	R	E	S	S		H	E	D	Y		S	A	E
H	U	T	S		S	I	D	E		B	U	Y	S
E	R	E		H	U	D		C	A	R	E	T
D	E	D	U	C	E	D		T	R	A	G	E	D	Y
		S	O	R	A		R	O	B	E
F	I	R	E	M	E	N		I	S	O	L	A	T	E
E	N	E	R	O		R	C	A		D	E	N
A	I	L	S		I	D	E	E		S	O	R	E
S	T	A		E	R	I	C		B	E	A	R	E	R
T	I	P	O	V	E	R		M	O	R	N	I	N	G
	A	S	C	E	N	T		U	R	G	E	N	C	Y
	L	E	S	L	E	Y		G	E	O	R	G	E

Puzzle 1-35: St. Patrick's Day
Page 40

P	A	C	E	D		A	P	T		B	O	G	U	S
A	F	I	R	E		U	R	I		U	N	I	T	E
B	O	R	I	C		N	A	M		M	E	G	A	N
L	U	C	K	O	F	T	H	E	I	R	I	S	H	
O	L	E		D	E	J	A		O	A	F			
		C	E	D	E		G	N	P		S	P	A	
A	R	D	O	R		M	A	U	I		W	E	A	R
W	O	R	K	S	L	I	K	E	A	C	H	A	R	M
A	L	O	E		I	M	A	S		R	I	L	E	Y
Y	E	P		B	E	A		T	R	A	P			
		D	U	G		P	L	U	M		A	B	U	
	H	O	R	S	E	S	H	O	E	F	A	L	L	S
P	A	N	A	M		O	L	D		U	R	I	A	H
I	V	A	N	A		D	O	G		L	E	A	S	E
X	E	N	O	N		A	X	E		L	A	S	E	R

Puzzle 1-36: On the Threshold
Page 41

P	H	I	L		M	C	S		D	O	T	H
R	I	C	A		E	O	N		E	P	E	E
O	R	E	M		D	O	O	R	B	E	L	L
M	E	S	A	B	I		B	A	R	R	E	D
		R	O	C	K		P	I	E			
D	O	O	R	N	A	I	L		S	T	L	O
I	R	V		N	I	L	O	T		T	A	P
P	E	E	R		D	O	O	R	W	A	Y	S
		R	E	A		S	K	U	A			
E	N	C	A	M	P		E	E	R	I	E	R
D	O	O	R	Y	A	R	D		M	O	V	E
G	R	A	M		S	O	U		E	W	E	S
E	A	T	S		T	O	P		R	A	N	T

Puzzle 1-37: Going Down!
Page 42

```
R E B A   P O L A R   R A S H
I R O N   A W A R E   H I L O
S I N K O R S W I M   E D A M
K N E A D     D I C T A T E
      R E B E L   S A O
L P G A   A M A   S U R E S T
A U R   C R I S T   C I S C O
D R O P I N T H E B U C K E T
L I V E N   S I N E S   E N E
E M E N D S   N O D   B R E D
      D E N   G R E T A
A R E A R U G     A L T E R
M O R N   F A L L I N L O V E
O M I T   F L O A T   A R E S
S E E S   S E N D S   D E N T
```

Puzzle 1-38: Keeping Time
Page 43

```
R O T A   A M A N A   O G R E
E R N S   G O R E S   C R E W
S E T H T H O M A S   E A S E
      S A D   T E N A N T S
D E C   A S S   M E N D
E X H O R T   C A B S   F E D
B I R D S   F A U L T   A L I
A L O E   M A R R Y   S T L O
T E N   A O R T A   A S H E N
E D O   O N E S   A S T E R N
   M O N A   C B S   R Y E
T E E T E R S   A A A
A L T A   C L E P S Y D R A E
P I E R   H A V R E   R I L E
E E R Y   S T E A D   Y A L E
```

Puzzle 1-39: Tricky Twosomes
Page 44

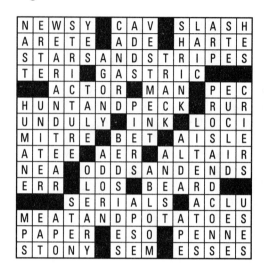

```
N E W S Y   C A V   S L A S H
A R E T E   A D E   H A R T E
S T A R S A N D S T R I P E S
T E R I   G A S T R I C
      A C T O R   M A N   P E C
H U N T A N D P E C K   R U R
U N D U L Y   I N K   L O C I
M I T R E   B E T   A I S L E
A T E E   A E R   A L T A I R
N E A   O D D S A N D E N D S
E R R   L O S   B E A R D
      S E R I A L S   A C L U
M E A T A N D P O T A T O E S
P A P E R   E S O   P E N N E
S T O N Y   S E M   E S S E S
```

Puzzle 1-40: Rhyme Theme
Page 45

```
A L O H A   C R A N E   I V E
S E D A N   H O S E A   N E D
H E D D A H O P P E R   T H E
E R E   R A K E S   S H E E N
S Y R   C H E   T H E R M
      S H A R E C R O P P E R
C H A R Y   N E A T   R N A
H I F I   B L E E P   S E C T
A G T   R E A R   R I T E S
T H E B I G B O P P E R
   T R I P S   I R E   A G E
F A L D O   L E G A L   P E R
L I I   S H O W S T O P P E R
E L F   T E N E T   F A L S E
E S E   E M E R Y   F R E E D
```

Puzzle 1-41: In the Papers
Page 46

Puzzle 1-42
Page 47

Puzzle 1-43: Spare Parts
Page 48

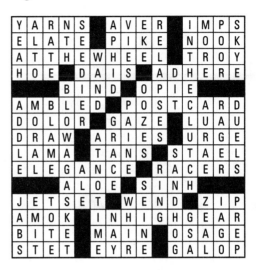

Puzzle 1-44: Sound Comparison
Page 49

Puzzle 1-45: Petrified Forest

Page 50

```
J A D E . F A C E . S M E L T
O G R E . E C O N . C O T T A
B O U L D E R C O L O R A D O
. . . A L I A . A W E . . . .
C H A R M E D . D U L L A R D
R E N O I R . G A R S . R U E
I R A T E . S A V E . M A S S
. S T O N E P H I L L I P S .
T H O R . S L A T . E M A I L
S E L . S C A N . R A S H A D
E Y E S H O T . C A N Y O N S
. . A E R . A R C O . . . . .
R O C K E T S C I E N T I S T
E L L E N . C H E R . I D E A
C A U S A . H E S S . C O A X
```

Puzzle 1-47: You Name It

Page 52

```
R A P I D . B O Y S . B O W .
A M A N A . H O R S T . O H O
M O L L Y C O D D L E . B A T
P R E A C H E S . . L I B R A
. . A I R . M A L A Y A N . .
I N P A R T . J A P A N S . .
D I A N E . F U R O R . O O O
I N D Y . C O M E S . A X E L
G E D . P O O P S . T R E N D
. Y E A R L Y . M A C R O S .
U P W A R D S . D O N . . . .
R I A T A . O R A T O R I O .
G A G . D O N N Y B R O O K S
E N O . E D I T S . U N M E T
S O N . R E P O . M A S S E .
```

Puzzle 1-46

Page 51

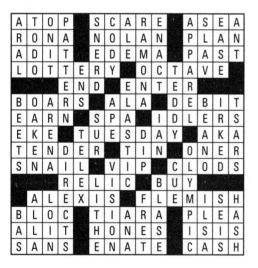

```
A T O P . S C A R E . A S E A
R O N A . N O L A N . P L A N
A D I T . E D E M A . P A S T
L O T T E R Y . O C T A V E .
. . E N D . E N T E R . . . .
B O A R S . A L A . D E B I T
E A R N . S P A . I D L E R S
E K E . T U E S D A Y . A K A
T E N D E R . T I N . O N E R
S N A I L . V I P . C L O D S
. . R E L I C . B U Y . . . .
. A L E X I S . F L E M I S H
B L O C . T I A R A . P L E A
A L I T . H O N E S . I S I S
S A N S . E N A T E . C A S H
```

Puzzle 1-48: Army Docs

Page 53

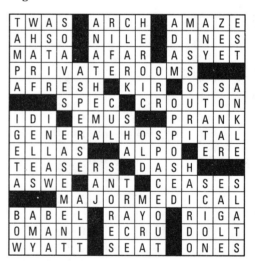

```
T W A S . A R C H . A M A Z E
A H S O . N I L E . D I N E S
M A T A . A F A R . A S Y E T
P R I V A T E R O O M S . . .
A F R E S H . K I R . O S S A
. . S P E C . C R O U T O N .
I D I . E M U S . P R A N K .
G E N E R A L H O S P I T A L
E L L A S . A L P O . E R E .
T E A S E R S . D A S H . . .
A S W E . A N T . C E A S E S
. . M A J O R M E D I C A L .
B A B E L . R A Y O . R I G A
O M A N I . E C R U . D O L T
W Y A T T . S E A T . O N E S
```

Puzzle 1-49: Separated at Birth
Page 54

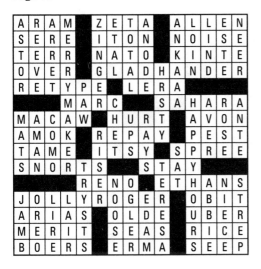

```
M I E S █ E B A N █ P A S T A
E T C H █ L O L A █ A S T A R
T C H A I K O V S K Y F A L K
S H O R T █ M A T E █ O N E S
█ █ P E P E █ Y E L L █ █
L U V █ M O R T █ P A L L E T
A N O N █ E A R L █ M O O R E
M C C A R T N E Y N E W M A N
B L A M E █ G E R E █ S A S E
S E L E N A █ S I A M █ N E T
█ █ S O R T █ C R A M █ █
A R E A █ L E O I █ Z A P P A
P I C K F O R D S H E L L E Y
E M C E E █ R O T S █ T O T E
G E E S E █ E R S T █ A P E S
```

Puzzle 1-51
Page 56

```
P A N G █ S T A G █ R I O T S
O V A L █ O R L E █ E N D U E
S I T U A T I O N █ A V E R T
S L U M P █ T H E S P I A N S
E A R █ P L E A █ L E O █
█ A B L E █ A I R L E S S
H E L L E S P O N T █ A C H E
O D I E █ O W E █ B O O N
L I Z A █ C O N T R O L L E D
E T E R N A L █ O L E O █
█ I O N █ M A T E █ G O A
T A R N I S H E S █ I V I N S
A R I E S █ A L I E N I S T S
L A P S E █ L O D E █ S T O A
C R E S S █ O N E R █ E S P Y
```

Puzzle 1-50: All Smiles
Page 55

```
A R A M █ Z E T A █ A L L E N
S E R E █ I T O N █ N O I S E
T E R R █ N A T O █ K I N T E
O V E R █ G L A D H A N D E R
R E T Y P E █ L E R A █
█ M A R C █ S A H A R A
M A C A W █ H U R T █ A V O N
A M O K █ R E P A Y █ P E S T
T A M E █ I T S Y █ S P R E E
S N O R T S █ S T A Y █
█ R E N O █ E T H A N S
J O L L Y R O G E R █ O B I T
A R I A S █ O L D E █ U B E R
M E R I T █ S E A S █ R I C E
B O E R S █ E R M A █ S E E P
```

Puzzle 1-52: School Days
Page 57

```
F A C E S █ L A S S O █ O H M
A D O R E █ A C T O R █ C E O
D E L I C A T E S U B J E C T
█ D E E M E D █ A L T I
E L F █ D I X █ L E T G O O F
P I E C E S █ F O R E █ T R S
A M E R █ G R A I L S █
█ A T O U C H O F C L A S S █
█ P R E E N S █ N A M E
S H H █ G E N T █ M A G N E T
N E A R E S T █ F A X █ D E C
A C T E █ P U R I S T █
P A R F O R T H E C O U R S E
I T E █ P E R I L █ M E A R A
N E D █ T O I L S █ S T P A T
```

Puzzle 1-53
Page 58

Puzzle 1-55: Calorie Counting
Page 60

Puzzle 1-54: Heavily Seasoned
Page 59

Puzzle 1-56: Recreational Real Estate
Page 61

Puzzle 1-57: Big Brother
Page 62

A	L	L	S		F	A	C	E	T		S	H	A	H
M	O	O	T		A	R	O	M	A		A	I	R	E
O	R	W	E	L	L	C	H	A	R	A	C	T	E	R
R	E	E	V	E	S		N	I	T	S		I	N	D
		E	T	E	S		L	A	K	O	T	A	S	
B	A	R		S	T	E	T		R	I	P			
A	L	A	R		T	A	R	A		N	E	R	D	S
B	E	N	E	V	O	L	E	N	T	G	R	O	U	P
E	X	T	R	A		S	A	D	A		A	R	N	O
	A	L	T		D	E	B	T		Y	E	T		
M	A	N	N	E	R	S		S	L	O	B			
A	L	I		T	O	T	E		O	R	E	L	S	E
J	A	N	I	S	J	O	P	L	I	N	B	A	N	D
O	M	E	N		A	V	O	I	D		O	L	E	O
R	O	S	S		N	E	S	T	S		P	O	E	M

Puzzle 1-59: Basic Grammar
Page 64

O	R	R	S		A	D	E	S	T	E		C	O	D
R	E	A	P		S	E	M	P	E	R		O	D	E
E	X	P	R	E	S	S	I	O	N	S		N	E	E
			E	A	T		G	U	N		S	C	A	M
A	L	T	A	R		O	R	T		A	L	E		
R	E	A	D		T	U	E	S		B	A	R	G	E
E	B	B		E	R	R	S		S	Y	N	T	A	X
T	R	U	D	G	E	S		P	A	S	T	I	M	E
E	U	L	O	G	Y		J	O	G	S		N	O	R
S	N	A	R	E		E	A	S	E		C	A	N	T
	T	A	D		N	I	T		B	A	S	E	S	
S	P	I	N		K	R	A		S	I	R			
L	O	O		D	I	A	L	E	C	T	I	C	A	L
E	R	N		A	L	P	A	C	A		N	O	D	E
Y	E	S		P	O	T	I	O	N		G	O	O	D

Puzzle 1-58: Patriotic Folks
Page 63

L	E	A	D	S		A	H	E	M		O	N	U	S
E	L	T	O	N		N	O	R	A		W	A	N	T
A	L	O	N	E		N	E	R	D		E	T	T	E
S	A	M	U	E	L	A	D	A	M	S		H	I	E
		T	R	I			T	E	A	B	A	L	L	
T	O	E	S		S	C	R	A	N	T	O	N		
A	R	T		P	E	A		S	A	H	I	B		
L	E	H	I		S	O	B	E	R		S	A	T	E
C	L	A	R	A		B	R	A			L	I	L	
	N	O	T	A	R	I	E	S		P	E	S	T	
G	R	A	N	I	T	E		P	A	L				
O	I	L		T	H	O	M	A	S	P	A	I	N	E
T	A	L	E		E	P	E	E		R	I	L	E	D
I	T	E	M		N	E	A	R		E	N	L	A	I
T	A	N	S		A	N	N	O		S	T	Y	L	E

Puzzle 1-60: Uniformly Distributed
Page 65

S	L	E	P	T		F	A	D	S		A	T	T	Y
T	E	P	E	E		A	L	E	C		S	H	E	A
O	C	E	A	N		V	O	T	E		T	E	A	K
W	H	E	R	E	D	O	G	E	N	E	R	A	L	S
			S	T	I	R		R	E	D	O			
B	I	O		S	N	I	P	S		G	N	A	S	H
E	N	D	S		G	T	O		P	E	O	R	I	A
K	E	E	P	T	H	E	I	R	A	R	M	I	E	S
A	R	T	E	R	Y		N	A	L		Y	O	G	I
A	T	S	E	A		A	T	B	A	T		T	E	T
		C	C	L	I		E	C	H	O				
I	N	T	H	E	I	R	S	L	E	E	V	I	E	S
S	A	R	I		M	A	I	A		B	I	T	T	E
L	E	A	F		A	C	T	I		A	N	T	O	N
E	S	P	Y		S	E	E	S		N	E	O	N	S

© American Puzzle Tournament

Puzzle 1-61
Page 66

```
S O L E _ D A R E D _ B L A H
E D E N _ A L I N E _ O O N A
T E N D _ Z E B R A _ R O N S
A S S U R E S _ A L A S K A _
_ _ R O D _ O P T I C _ _ _
A L B E E _ R U T _ S H E E T
G A R S _ H I T _ U L T I M A
O P A _ D I O C E S E _ D E R
R A N G E S _ A V E _ B E N T
A Z T E C _ S S E _ H E R D S
_ _ T R A C T _ M O A _ _ _
_ P L A Y E R _ C O I N A G E
A R O W _ S A B E R _ B O O T
N O L A _ O P A L S _ A N O N
A D A Y _ P E A L E _ G E N A
```

Puzzle 1-63: Hot Times
Page 68

```
P O P U P _ P A A R _ N E R D
A R E N A _ E S T E _ O M O O
M E L T I N G P O T _ S A N D
_ _ L O N E _ S M A S H I N G
A B M _ T O R _ S I T _ L I E
P R E _ S N E E _ N O I S E S
T A L C _ A L T E R S _ _ _
_ G L O B A L W A R M I N G _
_ _ M A M M A L _ S E E D
A D S O R B _ Y E A R _ W R Y
L O A _ N U N _ S T A _ S E E
E M B O S S E D _ R I O S _
P A I D _ H E A T I N G P A D
P I N E _ E D N A _ E L O P E
O N E S _ D Y A N _ D E T E R
```

Puzzle 1-62: Curious Crossbreeds
Page 67

```
A L S O R A N _ D I N G B A T
H E C T A R E _ O P E R A T E
A N A H E I M _ L A T I N O S
B O L E _ S O I L S _ P E P S
_ _ E R L E _ T A S T E _ _
P A S S E _ P A R _ O D D E R
O L D _ V A L _ M O O _ R E O
A G O _ E V A _ A W L _ E R A
C A W _ L E T _ R N A _ S I S
H E N C E _ E L K _ T V S E T
_ _ A D A G E _ C E O S _ _
F R O M _ C L O S E _ I H A D
L O R E T T A _ P L A C I D O
A L L U R E S _ A L T E R E D
K E Y P A D S _ T O A S T E D
```

Puzzle 1-64: Get Physical
Page 69

```
P A C T _ B E G E T _ O S L O
A S H E _ S T O R Y _ A W A Y
R A I N _ A C T U P _ T E S S
A B N E R _ H O P E C H E S T
S O R T O F _ T A O _ T I E
O N E _ N O O K S _ R I S E R
L U S T _ R D A _ U F O _ _
_ S T E A M E R T R U N K S _
_ _ L P S _ M A G _ A N T S
C A K E S _ L A T E R _ E R E
A R A _ E S E _ D E M E A N
L O V E S E A T S _ V A D I S
L U N A _ U N I T S _ R E N O
U S E S _ S T E A K _ L E E R
P E R T _ S O R R Y _ O P R Y
```

Puzzle 1-65: Exit Lines

Page 70

```
M A M A | C A R O L | S N I P
A B E S | A C U R A | P E D I
C A R P E N T E R S | R I O T
A S I | L I E S | S P I L L S
W E T L A N D | T O O T S |
| A T E | B R E E Z I L Y
W H E R E | C O U R T | M O E
H E L D | S A X E S | L O O N
O A T | M O P E S | C E N T S
A T O N E F O R | S H E |
| N E S T S | C H A R M E R
R A J A H S | N O R M | O N E
A L O T | P H I L I P R O T H
K O H L | O A K E N | A S E A
E E N Y | T H E S E | H E R B
```

Puzzle 2-1: Words You Know

Page 72

```
A C M E | I M P S | A C R E | C A P A
X R A Y | N E A T | F L E X | E B O N
E A S E | E R I E | R I D E | N E O N
S P H I N X | D E N I M | R A T T L E
| N I P S | P I C A | T I E |
S I N G L E T S | T A X I | T R E N D
O N E | E R R O R | N E S T S | M A E
I T E M | T I N E S | S L Y | A I D E
L O D E S | P A L E S | E P I G R A M
| R A N | R I V A L | E R E |
T R A C T O R | C E R E S | E N V O Y
H O L Y | S E C | R I A L S | T I D E
A L A | T E N O R | S P I T E | N O N
T E R R A | O X E N | S C I S S O R S
| E T E | S P O T | E L S E |
S U R T A X | W O M E N | T E X A N S
A R E A | P E A R | P O L O | T R E E
I S A K | E X I T | I V A N | I L E X
D A L E | L E N S | D A Y S | C O T Y
```

Puzzle 2-2: Vocabulary Building

Page 74

```
G E N E   S I T E   P A L M   S A M E
U S E S   A R A L   A R E A   Q U I P
S P A T   V O L U N T E E R   U N T O
T Y P H O O N   S O T   R E B A T E S
      E R R   K I T E D   S E L
S L A T E   D I V I D E D   E L C I D
L O S E   V I D E O   N O D   S O R E
O F T   W E E D   N O I S E S   C E N
E T E S I A N   I S L E   S T U R D Y
      R O N D E L S   P R O P O S E
R H O N D A   A L E E   T O R N A D O
A I D   Y R E K A N   S H I M   T O P
T R I O   S R O   C R E E L   S O R A
S E A N S   A T E L I E R   M U R A L
      S A D   A T O M S   H O N
C A S H I E R   A S P   C Y C L O N E
E C H O   C O M P E L L E D   E L I A
S T A R   A L O E   E A S E   S I R S
T A M E   L E T S   D O S S   S O O T
```

Puzzle 2-3: Expansion Teams

Page 76

```
T R Y O N   I C A M E   F O C I   M A R
B A O B A B   N O T E S   I R O N   O R E
S L U I C E   A L T O S   D I O N   N I M
P E R T H A M B O Y W O N D E R S   T O O
      S T R A I N S   A L L S   P E S T
A N E   A Y N   S A V E S   P U R E E
C A R L S B A D A P P L E S   S O M E
T H R I L L S   C R A B S   P A P A Y A S
      N Y E   O H O   L E T O   G U M
J E R K   I D E A S   S E R I F   U T E
A R E   M A C O N M I S C H I E F   N O L
C A N   A D O R E   R U R A L   P S S T
O T O   S I N S   P E R   A C E
B O B C A T S   F A U R E   I N O R D E R
      R I D S   N O R M A N C O N Q U E S T
R E A T A   M O N K S   O N O   I C E
E R I E   L A N D   H O W I T I S
S A N   T U S C A L O O S A C A N N O N S
U S E   O R S O   A R B O R   T A I P E I
M E R   D E E M   S C O L D   E L D E R S
E D S   O D D S   S A S E S   L E R O I
```

Puzzle 2-4: Gourmet Treats

Page 78

Puzzle 2-5: Separated at Birth

Page 80

Puzzle 2-6: Whose Movie Is This?

Page 82

```
Z A P P A ▪ L I S T ▪ T R A D E ▪ S T A S
A B E A M ▪ E L I A ▪ R E V E L ▪ T A T E
G U L L I V E R S T R A V E L S ▪ E T O N
S T E M ▪ I D E A T E ▪ R A E ▪ R A M A
▪ ▪ E D S ▪ L O S S E S ▪ R E M I T
▪ E B O L A ▪ S O P H I E S C H O I C E
T R E S T L E S ▪ O E N ▪ T O O ▪ ▪
R A T S O ▪ S T E R N A ▪ P O P ▪ T E L L
U L Z A N A S R A I D ▪ A R M ▪ E E R I E
▪ ▪ P E A R L ▪ B R I A N S S O N G
A P O G E E ▪ T I E ▪ E R S ▪ E C H O E S
H O W A R D S E N D ▪ G A O L S ▪ ▪
E L E M I ▪ E G G ▪ W A Y N E S W O R L D
M E S A ▪ A N Y ▪ R I N S E S ▪ A H E A D
▪ ▪ A G A ▪ B U G ▪ R E T R I E V E
C H A R L O T T E S W E B ▪ A N O D E
H O T E L ▪ E T H A N E ▪ E I S ▪ ▪
E T T E ▪ T E D ▪ M E T I N G ▪ I R I S
W A I L ▪ A L I C E S R E S T A U R A N T
E I R E ▪ U S U A L ▪ G L E E ▪ Z A I R E
D R E D ▪ T A M P A ▪ Y S E R ▪ I N N E R
```

Puzzle 2-7: Pet Shop

Page 84

```
A L E N E ▪ M A A M ▪ R E A P ▪ S C O W L
B E S O T ▪ I L K A ▪ E M I T ▪ H A N O I
C A T B U R G L A R ▪ H O R S E O P E R A
S P E E D E R S ▪ I N I T S ▪ L O O S E R
▪ ▪ L E N A ▪ S N O R E ▪ L U F T ▪
B I B I ▪ E N S L A V E ▪ L A D L E F U L
A P I S H ▪ T I A R A ▪ L A C E Y ▪ I T E
B A R T E R ▪ S N A K E E Y E S ▪ A S T A
A N D ▪ M O I S T ▪ E V E S ▪ O C H E R
S A W S ▪ S L Y ▪ B A R E R ▪ C H E E R Y
▪ A P R I L ▪ N A D I R ▪ C A M R Y ▪
A C T I V E ▪ R E L E E ▪ S U B ▪ B E D S
L A C K S ▪ B O A S ▪ E L M E R ▪ L O A
A S H E ▪ D O G P A D D L E ▪ R E G E N T
R T E ▪ C E R E S ▪ R U L E D ▪ S U N N I
M E R C A T O R ▪ L I M I T E D ▪ I S E E
▪ O V E N ▪ J E E P S ▪ B E A D ▪ ▪
F R A M E S ▪ M E A D S ▪ S U L T A N A S
R A B B I T E A R S ▪ T U R T L E N E C K
O C E A N ▪ T Y K E ▪ E T T E ▪ A C A R E
M E E T S ▪ S A Y S ▪ R E A D ▪ M E L E E
```

Puzzle 2-8: Connubial Comment
Page 86

Puzzle 2-9: Phun Phor All
Page 88

Puzzle 2-10: Diamond Jubilee

Page 90

Puzzle 2-11: Whereabouts

Page 92

Puzzle 2-12

Page 94

D	R	I	P	S		O	L	D	E		G	E	M	S		A	S	T	R	O
R	E	M	I	T		N	A	I	L		E	D	I	E		R	E	H	E	M
S	C	A	L	E	N	E	T	R	I	A	N	G	L	E		C	A	R	V	E
		L	A	Y	N	E			T	E	A	K		D	O	R	E	E	N	
B	A	B	B	L	E	D		M	B	A		R	E	B	A		C	E	L	S
A	L	O	U		B	O	E	R		R	A	N	C	H	O					
K	I	N	G	G	E	O	R	G	E	I	I	I		R	A	H		F	B	S
E	T	A		E	A	S	I	E	R		C	O	D	E		I	M	A	R	I
		M	O	R	T	O	N		S	E	W	E	R		N	I	K	O	N	
A	R	T	I	S	T	E		S	O	D	A	S		L	A	D	I	N	G	
B	E	E	N		H	O	L	Y	T	R	I	N	I	T	Y		A	N	T	E
B	A	R	N	E	Y		Y	E	A	R	N		I	N	S	I	D	E	S	
E	L	C	I	D		M	E	A	T	Y		P	A	N	D	E	R			
S	T	E	E	D		E	S	S	O		G	O	R	G	O	N		K	E	N
S	Y	N		I	A	N		T	R	I	P	L	E	E	N	T	E	N	T	E
		T	S	E	T	S	E		R	A	Y	S			N	O	T	E		
S	M	E	E		T	A	S	S		A	S	P		S	P	A	T	T	E	R
M	A	N	T	R	A		T	H	E	N		T	O	R	S	I				
I	R	A	T	E		T	H	E	K	I	N	G	S	T	O	N	T	R	I	O
T	I	R	E	D		H	E	R	E		B	R	A	T		E	L	E	N	A
H	A	Y	E	S		O	R	E	S		A	E	R	O		R	E	A	D	S

Puzzle 2-13: Twofers

Page 96

M	A	N	O	R		I	C	E		R	A	S	P		A	H	A	B
A	D	O	R	E		N	O	M		O	V	E	R		P	A	L	L
P	A	R	A	D	I	G	M	S		N	E	R	O		O	B	I	E
	M	A	N		L	E	E		P	A	R	A	M	E	D	I	C	S
		G	E	L		D	A	I	S		O	R	A	T	E	S		
D	U	P	E	S		G	I	S	T		M	E	T	A	L			
A	T	A		P	A	R	A	P	H	R	A	S	E	S		P	A	W
R	A	R	E		C	A	N	S		O	N	E	R		S	A	T	E
C	H	A	N	G	E	S		N	A	G		S	E	C	R	E	T	
	P	O	I		P	A	R	A	D	O	X		T	O	A			
S	H	E	L	L	S		N	O	B		Y	I	E	L	D	E	D	
I	O	T	A		T	I	N	T		D	E	L	E		D	I	R	E
R	E	S		P	A	R	A	C	H	U	T	E	R	S		S	I	N
		D	A	T	E	S		A	D	I	M		A	G	E	N	T	
A	L	P	I	N	E		O	L	E	O		A	G	E				
P	A	R	A	G	R	A	P	H	S		L	E	D		N	E	D	
R	U	I	N		O	L	L	A		P	A	R	A	S	I	T	E	S
O	R	N	E		O	M	A	R		A	T	O		P	E	A	L	E
N	A	T	S		M	A	N	E		Y	E	S		A	S	S	E	T

Puzzle 2-14: Auto-Solving

Page 98

	V	E	E		P	A	P	A		L	E	A	P	A	T		M	U	M	S
S	I	M	P		A	L	A	S		E	N	T	I	C	E		I	T	A	L
T	R	E	E	T	R	U	N	K		S	T	I	L	T	S		S	A	N	A
I	N	N	E	R		M	I	E	N	S		C	L	U	T	C	H	H	I	T
R	A	D	I	A	N		C	R	E	E	P			P	E	R	M			
		S	C	O	P			D	E	C	A	F		R	O	A	D	I	E	
S	T	A	T	E	H	O	O	D		S	E	L	A			S	O	R	E	
C	O	B		O	L	D	E	S	T		C	A	R	T	W	H	E	E	L	
R	O	L	E		W	E	E	P	I	E	R		T	I	E	A				
A	B	A	S	H		T	O	G	A	E	D		S	T	R	A	F	E		
M	A	T	T	E	R	H	O	R	N		F	I	R	E	E	N	G	I	N	E
	D	E	E	D	E	E		T	E	N	U	T	A			S	A	N	E	R
		G	A	M	A		R	A	T	T	L	E	R		S	A	R	I		
S	P	A	R	E	P	A	R	T		P	E	O	P	L	E			L	G	E
T	O	R	E		N	E	A	P			S	H	I	F	T	K	E	Y	S	
S	T	E	W	E	D		S	T	O	I	C		S	E	R	A				
		A	L	A	N		I	N	U	S	E		R	I	P	E	N	S		
J	A	C	K	F	R	O	S	T		S	T	A	T	S		C	I	L	I	A
A	B	L	E		N	O	T	A	T	E		T	H	I	N	K	T	A	N	K
N	O	U	N		E	N	A	M	O	R		I	N	T	O		A	T	E	E
E	Y	E	S		R	E	G	E	N	T		N	O	E	L		L	E	S	

Puzzle 2-15: The Barber-y Coast

Page 100

C	A	R	E	W		S	T	A	T		L	A	P	S	E	S
O	P	E	R	A		C	O	R	A		A	L	O	H	A	S
M	I	N	I	S		H	O	A	X		N	I	C	E	S	T
B	E	A	C	H	C	O	M	B	I	N	G		K	A	Y	
O	C	T			A	L	E	S		O	U	T	E	R		
S	E	A	S	P	R	A	Y		B	R	O	A	D	W	A	Y
		L	A	I	R		P	E	D	R	O		A	V	A	
	S	C	O	R	N		C	A	N	I		I	T	E	M	
C	O	A	S	T	G	U	A	R	D	C	U	T	T	E	R	S
A	N	T	H		P	R	E	S		S	E	A	R	S		
B	I	C		U	S	H	E	R		B	U	L	L			
S	C	H	I	Z	O	I	D		O	A	R	L	O	C	K	S
	A	G	I	R	L		A	P	S	E		L	E	A		
T	W	O		C	L	I	P	P	E	R	S	H	I	P	S	
G	O	A	T	E	E		S	H	O	T		T	E	N	T	S
E	N	V	I	E	R		M	I	S	E		A	R	G	U	E
M	E	E	T	L	Y		E	D	E	N		G	A	S	P	S

Puzzle 2-16: What Kids Say
Page 102

```
S T R E W ■ C R A S S ■ T A S K
T R O P I C ■ A U R A S ■ R I T A
O U T S T A Y S T O U T ■ I S I S
P E S O ■ N A T H A N ■ R O L L E
■ M O O R ■ R A T E ■ E L M
C P A ■ P E D R O ■ S I N E W S
H A S H E S ■ E B B ■ L O L A
E T H A N ■ S T E E L E ■ T Y R E
S I T S ■ X R A Y R E X ■ O W E D
T O R S ■ A I R B A G ■ B R I G S
■ A L E X ■ D O T ■ C O O L I E
■ E Y E L I D ■ W E L L S ■ E S L
A R T ■ A S I A ■ I A N S
B O R O N ■ C L O S E R ■ E R A S
U T A H ■ E I G H T D A Y D A T E
S I S I ■ K E E N E ■ S E A S O N
E C H O ■ E R R O R ■ S N A P S
```

© American Puzzle Tournament

Puzzle 3-1
Page 106

CRUDE COGENT FACT: HE WHO IS WRAPPED UP IN HIMSELF MAKES A SMALL PACKAGE.

Puzzle 3-2
Page 106

ONE NINTH OF A FLOATING ICEBERG IS VISIBLE ABOVE THE SURFACE.

Puzzle 3-3
Page 106

PROSPEROUS DENTIST CLAIMS HE LEADS HAND TO MOUTH EXISTENCE — A PARADOX!

Puzzle 3-4
Page 107

WHILE MOST TOYS ARE GIVEN AWAY, YOYOS ALWAYS HAVE STRINGS ATTACHED.

Puzzle 3-5
Page 107

TRUE AND FALSE: NOT ONE SINGLE MAN AMONG MANY HUSBANDS.

Puzzle 3-6
Page 107

PHRASE "ALPHA TO OMEGA" MEANS SAME THING AS "FROM FIRST TO LAST."

Puzzle 3-7
Page 108

PANNED BY CRITICS, ROCK AND ROLL SINGER WEEPS EN ROUTE TO BANK.

Puzzle 3-8
Page 108

"THE ONLY DIFFERENCE BETWEEN CAPRICE AND A LIFELONG PASSION IS THAT THE FORMER LASTS LONGER." — OSCAR WILDE

Puzzle 3-9
Page 108

"THE REAL PROBLEM IS WHAT TO DO WITH PROBLEM-SOLVERS AFTER THE PROBLEMS ARE SOLVED." — GAY TALESE

Puzzle 3-10
Page 109

"I AM ONLY AN AVERAGE MAN BUT, BY GEORGE, I WORK HARDER AT IT THAN ANYONE ELSE." — THEODORE ROOSEVELT

Puzzle 3-11
Page 109

"THE SECRET OF RUNNING A GOOD BUSINESS IS TO KNOW SOMETHING NOBODY ELSE KNOWS." — ARISTOTLE ONASSIS

Puzzle 3-12

Page 110

"HAPPINESS IS HAVING A LARGE, LOVING, CLOSE-KNIT FAMILY LIVING IN ANOTHER CITY." — GEORGE BURNS

Puzzle 3-13

Page 110

"MY ADVICE TO ANY DIPLOMAT WHO WANTS TO HAVE A GOOD PRESS IS TO HAVE A FEW KIDS AND A DOG." — CARL ROWAN

Puzzle 3-14

Page 111

"IF THERE IS A DISPUTE BETWEEN A MUSICIAN AND MYSELF, IT IS SETTLED AMICABLY. I WIN!" — DANNY KAYE

Puzzle 3-15

Page 111

"THE KITCHEN IS A PLACE IN WHICH THERE ARE ALWAYS DISCOVERIES TO BE MADE." — GRIMOD DE LA REYNIERE

Puzzle 3-16

Page 112

"WHEN HUMAN BEINGS WERE ENDOWED WITH BRAINS, THEY DID NOT COME WITH A GUARANTEE." — BARON DE MONTESQUIEU

Puzzle 3-17

Page 112

"IF YOU HAVEN'T GOT ANYTHING NICE TO SAY ABOUT ANYBODY, COME SIT NEXT TO ME." — ALICE ROOSEVELT LONGWORTH

Puzzle 3-18: 15 x 15 Squares

Page 113

Puzzle 3-19: 17 x 15 Squares

Page 114

Puzzle 3-20

Page 115

```
O N   H I S   D E A T H   B E D   P O O R
L U B I N   L I E S   H I S   S P O U S E
I S   I N   D E S P A I R   W I T H   F R E
Q U E N T   C R I E S   A N D   M U T U A L
  S I G H S   T H E Y   B O T H   E X P R E
S S   T H E I R   C A R E   A   D I F F E R
E N T   C A U S E   S A Y S   P A R S O N
S L Y   T H E   S A M E   E F F E C T   M A
Y   G I V E   P O O R   L U B I N   F E A R
S   T H A T   H E   M A Y   D I E   H I S
W I F E   T H A T   H E   M A Y   L I V E
```

A PATCHOULI
B RHUMB
C INHOUSE
D OPIUM
E REDEEMED
F ATTESTS
G RUSHES
H EFFIGIES
I ALIVE
J SHEFFIELD
K OYSTERBAY
L NEEDLED
M ASPERSION
N BATHSHEBA
O LEAFY
P EXASPERATED
Q ASEA
R FROGPRINCE
S FINISH
T LYSISTRATA
U ISTHMUS
V CHIMNEY
W THATCH
X INQUISITIVE
Y OPRAH
Z NEWSWORTHY

Puzzle 3-21

Page 116

```
I   M I G H T   H A V E   B E E N   A   F A R M Y A
R D   H E N   S C R A T C H I N   I N   T H E   S U
N   T H E R E   M I G H T   H A V E   B E E N   A
C R O W D   O F   C H I C K S   A F T E R   M E   T
O   R U N   T H E R E   M I G H T   H A V E   B E E
N   A   C O C K E R E L   F I N E   T O   P A Y   U
S   H I S   R E S P E C T S   I N S T E A D   O F
S I T T I N   H E R E   T I L L   S O M E O N E   C
O M E S   A N D   W R I N G S   O U R   N E C K S
```

A PHASEDOWN
B ANTITHESES
C MATCHSTICK
D ARCHDIOCESE
E YEMENI
F RHONE
G ECHOCHAMBER
H SHUFFLE
I SUGGESTION
J OVERWROUGHT
K MAVERICK
L EDITHHEAD
M OLEAN
N FAINTER
O MEANING
P ENVIES
Q PATRICKRAFTER
R OBSCENITIES
S ENTHRONE
T TRENT
U RUMBLEFISH
V YACHTSMEN

Puzzle 3-22
Page 117

I	T		I	S		N	O	T		E	V	I	L		I	N		A	N	Y
	W	A	Y		T	H	A	T		I		C	A	N		J	U	D	G	E
	E	V	I	L		I	T	S		O	N	L	Y		F	A	U	L	T	
T	H	A	T		I		C	A	N		S	E	E		I	S		T	H	A
T		I	T		P	R	O	D	U	C	E	D		P	E	O	P	L	E	
W	H	O		D	I	D	N	T		L	O	V	E		H	E	R		E	N
O	U	G	H		P	E	O	P	L	E		W	H	O		W	O	U	L	D
	S	E	L	L		H	E	R		T	O		S	T	R	A	N	G	E	R
S		F	O	R		T	H	I	R	T	Y		P	I	E	C	E	S		O
F		S	I	L	V	E	R													

A PEPPERHASH
B AHHA
C TRAVELS
D CHILD
E OUTOFTHIS
F NEEDIER
G RAISIN
H OPTION
I YOUNGSTER
J PUDDLE
K RIGHTOFWAY

L INVITE
M NEWCASTLE
N COUCHPOTATO
O ENJOY
P ORWELL
Q FAULTY
R TWISTERS
S ILLDOIT
T DINGLE
U EVILTO
V SEVENTH

Appendix B
Working Non-Crossword Puzzles

In This Chapter
▶ Discovering cryptograms
▶ Giving some structure to diagramless puzzles
▶ Getting the lowdown on acrostics

*I*n this appendix, I show you how to work the puzzles you find in Part III, namely the cryptogram, diagramless, and acrostic.

Cracking the Cryptogram Code

Cryptograms are all about letter replacement. Letters in cryptograms have been switched around, creating a funky-looking message that you need to decipher.

In a cryptogram, every letter stands for a different one (and only one) throughout the message. For example, "B" may represent "T" through the cryptogram, and "T" may mean "C." Although the pattern of the sentence looks familiar, the "words" read as if they are in some kind of secret code.

The "code" changes from puzzle to puzzle, as though the alphabet flies up in the air, with the letters landing in different places, for each puzzle. Unfortunately, cracking the code on one puzzle doesn't give you a Rosetta Stone that you can apply to all other cryptograms.

Cryptogram words are exact replicas of the actual words they disguise. For example, if you see a three-letter word as part of a cryptogram, you know that a three-letter word appears in the quote or phrase hidden within the puzzle.

Typically, a cryptogram message is a quotation (complete with punctuation). The author's name may appear at the end of the cryptogram. Note that some cryptograms offer a hint by revealing the identity of one of the disguised letters. You may want to ignore the help, or you may welcome a helping hand until you get the hang of it.

To work the cryptogram, follow these steps:

1. **Jot down the alphabet on scrap paper.**

   You need to do a little prep work first. You use this list to keep tabs on the letters you have already matched up and, consequently, which letters are still "unused."

2. **Scan the cryptogram for one-letter words, which are typically A or I.**

   Of course, you won't know which of the letters is the right one until you work a little more into the puzzle, but if you have a good feeling about one letter over the other, go ahead and pencil it in.

A spooky alternative name haunts cryptograms

For short, puzzle heads refer to cryptograms — a bit ghoulishly — as *crypts*. Constructors are known as *cryptographers*.

---

3. **After you crack the code on a letter, pencil in all occurrences of that letter in the puzzle. For example, where you find L to replace A, identify all the A's as L's through the cryptogram.**

   And I do mean pencil! You may need to experiment many times before you actually match up a letter. Don't attempt to work a cryptogram with a pen unless you really enjoy the smell of corrector fluid.

4. **Scan the cryptograms for two-letter words, then three-letter words, and so on, matching letters up as you go.**

   With each grouping of words, the message should come more and more into focus.

Table B-1 lists the most common words that appear in cryptograms; the words in each length category are listed in frequency of appearance.

Table B-1	Cryptogram Repeaters
Number of Letters	*Repeaters*
1	A and I
2	IT, IN, IS, IF, AT, ON, TO, OF, AS, and AN
3	THE, AND, FOR, ARE, and BUT
4	THAT, THIS, THAN, and THEN

You also need to be on the lookout for the following patterns as you work your way through the cryptogram:

✔ **Apostrophes:** Where an apostrophe appears at the end of a word followed by a single letter, your choice is limited to S or T (or sometimes D). When it follows a single letter, that letter must be I to give you I'd, I'll, or I've. Where an apostrophe is followed by two letters, your choice opens to 'LL, 'RE, and 'VE.

✔ **Double letters:** Check for EE, OO, FF, LL, SS, TT, and MM, in that order.

✔ **Final letters:** Check for E, T, S, D, N, and R, in this order, at the end of words.

✔ **Initial letters:** Check for T, A, O, M, H, and W at the beginning of words.

✔ **Suffixes:** Check for ING and LY in longer words.

Some cryptograms aren't just fun and games

During World War II, the Germans sent messages to their various armed forces overseas through a hard-to-crack secret code called Enigma. The Allies recruited legions of cryptographers to break the code in order to get the inside information on what the Germans were planning. Indeed, after the Allies deciphered the code, the tide turned for the Axis nations and the world at large.

The cryptogram's alphabet may not contain all 26 letters of the standard alphabet, depending on which letters show up in the message. A cryptographer may try to confuse you by deliberately eliminating some letters from the message altogether.

The key to cryptogram decoding, according to Laura Z. Hobson, author of the classic novel *Gentleman's Agreement* as well as scores of cryptograms, is to bear in mind that the most commonly used letter in English is E. Experienced crypt solvers often begin the decoding process by looking for E first. The most popular consonant is T. After you determine which letters represent E and T, you can move on to the next group of commonly used letters. Expert consensus ranks O and S in that category. M follows, according to Hobson. Other runners-up are A, I, and N.

Attempting the Diagramless

One of the neat aspects of conventional crosswords is that you don't need any special equipment to play the game. As long as you have a writing utensil, you can play.

When you tackle the diagramless puzzle, however, you need some additional equipment. In a diagramless puzzle, you get Across and Down clues, but no grid to fill with the answers to the clues. Your job is to sketch out a grid (according to the dimensions shown at the top of the puzzle) by using the answers to the clues. Although some people solve the diagramless in their heads, most acrossionados like to see the grid on paper. Of course, you can use the back of an envelope in a pinch (I have). But in order to be sure that you're on the right square, you may need a supply of graph paper and a clean eraser.

Try to keep two sheets of graph paper handy while solving a diagramless puzzle. With the extra sheet, you have the opportunity to experiment as you try to uncover a general pattern.

Because you don't have a black-and-white grid pattern to look at, the first step in attempting the diagramless is to refer to the dimensions indicated at the top of the puzzle. The dimensions look like a math formula, as in "15 x 15." For a 15 x 15 puzzle, draw a frame that measures 15 squares across and down on your graph paper to help you focus on the emerging pattern.

Necessity was the mother of a new puzzle

A happy editorial oversight caused the development of the diagramless, or so Margaret Farrar, longtime puzzle editor at *The New York Times,* told me. The seed of this puzzle style sprouted at a luncheon in 1925 over a stack of crosswords. Margaret was convening with her collaborators, Prosper Buranelli and F. Gregory Hartswick, who were jointly responsible for the very first crossword puzzle collection, to review material for a future edition. When they found that a grid was missing from the manuscript, Hartswick sketched out a blank one on the back of a menu by following the clues. The group realized that they'd come upon a new angle on solving the standard crossword. They dubbed their creation the diagramless.

Some sources supply a blank grid for you on the page in the correct dimensions, so that all you have to do is carefully plot the pattern. However, you don't have a black-and-white grid to look at, so the next step in attempting the diagramless is to determine where to insert 1 Across on your graph paper.

Grids always measure an odd number of squares, such as 15 x 15 or 21 x 21. Patterns are mostly, but not always, symmetrical. Of course, if you discover that the pattern is symmetrical, solving is that much easier. For example, you can safely transfer the pattern on top to its corresponding area in the bottom corner.

(Diagramless patterns don't always conform to the typical symmetrical square patterns. Instead, the pattern may appear in curved shapes, such as a windmill or snowflake. Sometimes the grid for a diagramless is rectangular rather than square, as in 15 x 17. If the diagram isn't a square, the first number indicates the number of squares across, and the second number represents the number of squares down.)

Diagramless patterns usually incorporate more black squares into the grid than the standard crossword. That's how you may end up with a grid design that resembles a windmill or an X-shape. Naturally, the more unusual the pattern, the tougher the challenge becomes.

Your next step is to determine the length of the First Across entry. Unlike a crossword, you want to approach the diagramless from 1 Across for best results. Without a grid, you don't have that visual reference to how many letters are in each word and where the entries belong. Instead, you have two ways to determine how many letters appear in the 1 Across entry:

✔ Look at the number of the second Across clue. If it's 6, for example, then you can surmise that the entry for 1 Across contains five letters.

✔ Check that Down clues 1 through 5 don't appear in the Across column.

If the second Across clue is 6 Across, you know that the first word consists of five letters. The five Down clues, from 1 through 5, that don't have an Across function confirm your assumption.

How accurate the grid turns out to read is completely up to you: You have to use your pencil correctly for best results. Record each number in the corresponding grid square systematically as you work your way down the clues in order to keep track of the pattern. Fill in a black square to the left of and above each number that appears in both Across and Down columns.

What distinguishes 1 Across from every other Across clue is that the solver can be certain that each letter of its entry serves as the first letter of a Down entry. In this case, you can blacken the sixth square after filling in the Across entry. Insert the numbers 1 through 5 in the appropriate squares and try to solve as many of the first five Down clues as you can. Before long, you create a block of answers that sets the puzzle on its path.

Don't worry about the clues: Diagramless clues are simpler than those of the average crossword because the constructor doesn't want to compound the handicap.

Margaret Farrar, noted crossword expert, recommended practicing diagramlesses by working a regular crossword as a diagramless by folding over the grid. By trying this approach, you're guaranteed a 15 x 15 grid with a standard pattern, and you can get the hang of how the numbering system operates. Feel free to turn any crossword in this book into a diagramless.

Because diagramless puzzles don't usually follow the square shape of a crossword, you can't make assumptions about where answers fall in the grid until you have made some progress. But you do have some information on your side:

- ✔ **You know that the grid is usually symmetrical.** In most cases, the pattern on top is a mirror image of the bottom. After you have plotted the pattern for the top half, you can transfer it to the bottom, and the other way around, too. Less often, the symmetry is left to right.

- ✔ **You know that the second Across answer follows 1 Across somehow.** In the standard crossword (and in most diagramless puzzles), the second Across entry appears directly to the right of the first entry in the grid in the same line. But the diagramless makes an exception: The second Across entry may appear one line down and to the left of 1 Across. As entries emerge, you can determine where the second Across entry belongs in the grid.

What if the second Across clue doesn't appear in the Down column? If the 6 Across entry isn't included in the Down column, for example, your solving takes a different direction, because now you know that the second Across answer appears directly *below* 1 Across. Chances are that the answer to 6 Across may begin to emerge after you fill in some of the first five Down entries. If the second Across number also appears in the Down column along with two more Down clues, then it most likely appears to the right of 1 Across, following the typical crossword format. Following the example, 6 appears in both Across and Down, while 7 and 8 are only clued Down. The third Across clue, then, is 9.

Even before you proceed with the second Across answer, I recommend jotting down any answers that pop out at you next to the lists of clues. Scanning all the way through the Across and Down clues and writing down as many entries as you can beside the clues is helpful. Islands of answers may emerge this way. Sometimes you can solve separate parts of the puzzle and unite them later. Only confirmed acrossionados try to discern the pattern before working the clues. The fun of the diagramless lies in coordinating the two as you solve.

Every entry that appears in both the Across and Down columns in a diagramless has a black square to its left and above it. Every entry that appears only in the Down clues has a black square above it and below its final letter.

After you see a black-and-white pattern start to emerge at the top part of your graph, you can safely turn your grid upside down and sketch in the mirror image below. In fact, if you find the entries easier to solve at the bottom, you may want to approach the diagramless from the bottom.

Solving an Acrostic

A truly great puzzle is not only fun, but also enlightening. When you solve an acrostic puzzle, you can be 100 percent sure that you will discover something new, because books are the fodder of this literary puzzle.

Rather than a random collection of words, the grid contains an excerpt from a written work. Entries in the grid only read across, not down, moving from top row to bottom, reading left to right. Additionally, when you read the initial letters of the answer words in your word list from top to bottom, they spell out the author and title of the work that is quoted in the grid.

Technically, the double aspect of the acrostic describes the way the two basic elements of the puzzle interact. You work with the same two variables of the crossword — the grid and clues — but in a new way. You use a two-part solving process for an acrostic:

1. **First, you have to solve the clues in the word list.**

   The clues are not hard at all. In fact, in the case of a missing word, the acrostic constructor may cite the source. Instead of numbers, you find the word list (about two dozen words) sorted by letters from A through Z.

2. **Next, you transfer the letters you have so far from the word list into their assigned squares in the grid.**

   Every letter serves in the grid as well as in an answer on the word list. As you fill in the word list, you note a number beneath each letter that indicates its placement in the grid. The initial letters of each answer in the word list spell out the name of the author and title of the work quoted in the grid. After you fill in the squares, a quotation of about 25 words emerges as you read the grid from left to right.

Keep an eye on the initial letters as you make progress on solving the word list. When you see the beginnings of a name emerge, as in AL*R*DL*RDT*N*YS*N, you can take the leap and fill in ALFRED LORD TENNYSON. Recognizing the author's name helps you by giving you the first letters to the words in the word list.

Black squares in the acrostic grid serve as spaces between words. Every white square contains a number and letter, which corresponds to a letter in one of the words in the word list.

The following guidelines should give you a leg up on solving an acrostic:

- ✔ Acrostic grids read across only.
- ✔ Grids are rectangular and don't conform to any pattern.
- ✔ Clues are organized alphabetically rather than numbered.
- ✔ Clues are always straightforward definitions.
- ✔ Clues never have themes or relate to the final solution of the acrostic.
- ✔ The solver first fills in the answer words on dashes next to the clues.
- ✔ Each answer letter has an assigned number that corresponds to a square in the grid.
- ✔ The solver transfers the letters of each answer to their assigned squares.
- ✔ Black squares indicate the end of a word.
- ✔ Entries may start at the far right and end in the row below at the far left.

What's in a name?

The acrostic goes by a number of names, including the *double crostic, anacrostic, wordagram,* and *quoteword.* The name just depends upon which publication you're solving in.

Crossword editor and author Norman Hill remarks that the term *double cross* comes dangerously close to

sounding like *Double Crostic,* the original brand name of this game. In Hill's opinion, the acrostic blends the best elements of wordplay — the crossword, anagram, and trivia quiz — plus a dash of mystery.

The acrostic clues don't contain any tricks: They are completely straightforward. If you look up the answers in the dictionary, you find yourself staring right at the clues. In looking at a typical acrostic, for example, you find that the constructor pulls no punches. When a clue reads "Unsteady" followed by six dashes, the answer is a commonly used synonym like WOBBLY. When the answer in a word list consists of more than one word, the constructor indicates that fact in parentheses, as in "Insectivore, also called potamogale (2 wds)" for OTTER SHREW. In the case of a missing word, the puzzle maker always cites the source. When the quotation comes from Shakespeare, for example, the constructor lists the specific act and scene — the easier to look it up, if you want to.

The only trick about acrostic clues lies in the way you interpret the clue. When you have a clue such as "Thumb" followed by nine dashes, do you stare at your fingers, or do you take it for a verb, as in HITCHHIKE? Words from acrostic clues are in the dictionary, but you may have to move beyond the first definitions.

Words in the quotation may run on into two rows. The beginning of a word may appear on one line at the far right, while the final letters appear in the next line below to the far left. That split includes words of one syllable, as in TH on the top line and ERE on the next line, below and to the left, to read as THERE. Only a black square indicates the end of the word, not the outside frame of the grid, as per the standard crossword.

Puzzle people get creative with acrostics

Pulitzer Prize-winning puzzler Russell Baker *(Growing Up)* used to measure his solving prowess against the time he took to smoke one cigarette after lunch. Eventually, he traded in his addiction to smoking for that of working the acrostic. He may throw away an unfinished crossword, but with acrostics he returns to the grid — with a different pen in hand. The different color ink helps him measure how far he got with each attempt. On the rare occasion that he uses references, his favorites are *The World Almanac* and the *Information Please Almanac.* To Baker, puzzles are a form of mental relaxation and a great warm-up exercise before he gets down to his business as a journalist and author.

Elizabeth Kingsley: Creator of a newer, harder puzzle

The Double Crostic made its debut in the pages of the *Saturday Review of Literature* (later known as the *Saturday Review*) in March 1934. This puzzle format was the brainchild of a former English teacher from Brooklyn.

During a college reunion at Wellesley, Elizabeth Kingsley had an epiphany about how to improve the crossword puzzle. Dismayed by the popularity on campus of modern writers such as James Joyce and Gertrude Stein, Kingsley put her mind on keeping the classics alive. By working literary excerpts into the grids, she recognized a way to realize her goal.

For clues, she turned to her anagram letters (which are much like Scrabble tiles). By spelling out the quotation with the anagram letters, she could then scramble the letters together and rearrange them. To create the clues, she selected the letters in the author's name and the title of the work and set them in first place down the line.

In her original instructions, Kingsley underscored that "Up and down the letters mean nothing! The black squares indicate ends of words; therefore, words do not necessarily end at the right side of the diagram."

After retiring from the magazine at the end of 1952, the *Saturday Review* hailed Kingsley as "Her D-C Majesty" (also known as "Our Queen Elizabeth") and credited her with having "resuscitated more poets and essayists lost through the centuries than all the English I classes in the U.S.A. combined." She passed the baton over to Doris Nash Wortman, who carried on for 15 years until her death. Since the 1960s, the byline associated with the acrostic is Thomas H. Middleton.

The empty grid can give you some helpful hints about the way the sentence unfolds:

- **Single-letter words:** When you see a white square between two black squares, the two obvious choices in the English language are A and I. (On the rare occasion, you may come across an initial, as in "J. D." Salinger.) If multiple single-letter words appear in the grid, odds are that the excerpt is in the first person, and you can safely insert I in various parts of each place.

- **Three-letter words:** Most often, you're looking at THE or AND.

Although mainly familiar words comprise the acrostic word list, the occasional oddball obscure word does intrude. As Mrs. Kingsley wrote to a correspondent: "Do you realize that 'h's' are the bane of my existence, being as common as they are, and that 'h's' predominate in Greek, Hebrew, Hindu, and other Oriental words? If you were constructing a puzzle and had letters left over and they made a Vedic deity, what would you do?"

Index

●●●

Discover Dummies Online!

The Dummies Web Site is your fun and friendly online resource for the latest information about ...*For Dummies*® books and your favorite topics. The Web site is the place to communicate with us, exchange ideas with other ...*For Dummies* readers, chat with authors, and have fun!

Ten Fun and Useful Things You Can Do at www.dummies.com

1. Win free ...*For Dummies* books and more!
2. Register your book and be entered in a prize drawing.
3. Meet your favorite authors through the IDG Books Author Chat Series.
4. Exchange helpful information with other ...*For Dummies* readers.
5. Discover other great ...*For Dummies* books you must have!
6. Purchase Dummieswear™ exclusively from our Web site.
7. Buy ...*For Dummies* books online.
8. Talk to us. Make comments, ask questions, get answers!
9. Download free software.
10. Find additional useful resources from authors.

Link directly to these ten fun and useful things at **http://www.dummies.com/10useful**

For other technology titles from IDG Books Worldwide, go to **www.idgbooks.com**

Not on the Web yet? It's easy to get started with *Dummies 101*®: *The Internet For Windows*® *95* or *The Internet For Dummies*®, 4th Edition, at local retailers everywhere.

Find other ...*For Dummies* books on these topics:
Business • Career • Databases • Food & Beverage • Games • Gardening • Graphics
Hardware • Health & Fitness • Internet and the World Wide Web • Networking
Office Suites • Operating Systems • Personal Finance • Pets • Programming • Recreation
Sports • Spreadsheets • Teacher Resources • Test Prep • Word Processing

IDG BOOKS WORLDWIDE
BOOK REGISTRATION

Register This Book and Win!

We want to hear from you!

Visit **http://my2cents.dummies.com** to register this book and tell us how you liked it!

- ✔ Get entered in our monthly prize giveaway.

- ✔ Give us feedback about this book — tell us what you like best, what you like least, or maybe what you'd like to ask the author and us to change!

- ✔ Let us know any other *...For Dummies*® topics that interest you.

Your feedback helps us determine what books to publish, tells us what coverage to add as we revise our books, and lets us know whether we're meeting your needs as a *...For Dummies* reader. You're our most valuable resource, and what you have to say is important to us!

Not on the Web yet? It's easy to get started with *Dummies 101*®: *The Internet For Windows*® *95* or *The Internet For Dummies*®, 4th Edition, at local retailers everywhere.

Or let us know what you think by sending us a letter at the following address:

...For Dummies Book Registration
Dummies Press
7260 Shadeland Station, Suite 100
Indianapolis, IN 46256-3945
Fax 317-596-5498

BUSINESS AND GENERAL REFERENCE BOOK SERIES FROM IDG

COMPUTER BOOK SERIES FROM IDG